DON'T MISS THIS

IN THE DOCTRINE AND COVENANTS

DON'T MISS THIS

IN THE DOCTRINE AND COVENANTS

EXPLORING ONE VERSE FROM EACH SECTION

EMILY BELLE FREEMAN
and DAVID BUTLER

DESERET
BOOK

Salt Lake City, Utah

Library of Congress Cataloging-in-Publication Data

Names: Freeman, Emily Belle, author. | Butler, David, author.

Title: Don't miss this in The Doctrine and Covenants : exploring one verse from each section / Emily Belle Freeman and David Butler.

Description: Salt Lake City, Utah : Deseret Book, [2020] | Includes bibliographical references. | Summary: "Authors Emily Belle Freeman and David Butler continue their 'Don't Miss This' series by examining one critical verse in each section of the Doctrine and Covenants"—Provided by publisher.

Identifiers: LCCN 2020024876 | ISBN 9781629728094 (trade paperback)

Subjects: LCSH: Doctrine and Covenants—Commentaries. | LCGFT: Meditations.

Classification: LCC BX8628 .F74 2020 | DDC 289.3/23—dc23

LC record available at https://lccn.loc.gov/2020024876

Printed in the United States of America
Brigham Young University Press, Provo, UT

10   9   8   7   6   5   4   3   2   1

*To S. Michael Wilcox, whose powerful
testimony of the Restoration on a fall day in
the Sacred Grove strengthened mine.*

—EBF

*To Scott, whose friendship, insights, and
gifted scholarship have helped me discover treasure in
scripture I never would have found on my own.*

—DB

OUR HOPE FOR THIS BOOK

We don't know how you will use this book, but maybe it will help if we tell you how we use it. We leave it out near the kitchen table. We like to read one verse a day with its accompanying devotional at dinnertime and then talk about the question at the bottom while we eat. It is helping us to make the *Come, Follow Me* program part of our everyday routine.

This book is not meant to be a reference manual. It is more of a simple help for learners of all ages to find meaning in the scriptures by focusing on context, culture, and application. On some pages you will read the story from a historical point of view. On others you will meet one of the heroes of the Restoration. Sometimes we will share our own life experiences with applying insight from a particular verse or chapter. Hopefully the combination of all of these teaching techniques will help make your study of the Doctrine and Covenants more meaningful this year.

We absolutely love studying with you!

David and Emily

INTRODUCTION

Usually, if you sign up for a Church history tour, you know something about the Church whose tour it is. That was true for almost all of the forty-five people on our bus. There was just one who wasn't a member of our faith: Daniel, the bus driver. He knew nothing about our church when we met him outside the airport in Kansas City.

He didn't know what he was in for.

He had no idea that people would buy his dinner every night, or that everyone would jump in to help load the suitcases under the bus every time we started off (even though that was his job), or that he would be invited to come with us to visit every single site. That man with the gentle heart simply thought he would be driving a religious group across the country. He didn't know we would all be fast friends by the end.

We spent the week talking about Joseph and Emma, Oliver and Sidney, Hyrum and his mother, Lucy. He listened as he drove, and I'm sure he wondered what it was all about. On our first night in Nauvoo, he accompanied us for a walk down the "Trail of Hope." I told him about the Saints forced out of their homes during that cold February, many of whom walked down this street as they fled their city. He stopped to take a picture of the journal account of the woman who swept her entire house before she left.

"It's just like you described it was," he said, looking at me with compassion in his eyes. "I got a picture of that. I don't want to forget."

"It was a hard time for us," I told him.

"You know," he said, "when you don't know someone, you can be careless with them. And then you spend time with them, and they say, let me show you my Jesus. *My Jesus,*" he repeated, touching his heart. Then he looked at me carefully and said, "If they'd just spend time with you, they would know you know Him."

I thought of the dinners bought and the suitcases loaded and all the invitations extended to just come be with us. I thought about how many conversations had been filled with Jesus.

"I've driven religious groups for fourteen years," Daniel said as we got back to the bus, "and I've never driven a group like this one."

We gave him a gift at the end of the trip: a Book of Mormon signed by everyone on that bus, filled to bursting with words of gratitude and love for Daniel.

His reply?

"I was thinking to purchase one of these."

It is a Church history tour I will never forget.

We are about to start off on our own journey through the Doctrine and Covenants. We will talk about Joseph and Emma, Oliver and Sidney, Hyrum and his mother, Lucy. Those early Saints will become our travel companions, and we will become better for it. This journey will soften our hearts and strengthen our faith. It will give us glimpses of understanding and flashes of insight. We will discover the stories behind the sections and some of the ways God answers the simple questions of His people.

Just like Daniel, maybe we will take small snapshots in our minds of the things we don't want to forget.

This is a journey that will help us come to know the Lord.

It is interesting to study in detail the life of a prophet so many people question. Truly his name is had for good and evil around the world, even still today. Perhaps you wonder at the details of his story. Maybe you know some who have walked away in unbelief. Joseph himself once said, "I don't blame anyone for not believing my history. If I had not experienced what I have, I could not have believed it myself."[1]

There is something about walking through his story from beginning to end that instills a belief in its truth. We will see in Joseph an obscure boy, a stalwart husband, a doting father, a faithful friend, a loyal son, and a dedicated brother. We will also read of his faults, his doubts, and his failures. It is the combination of the two, the full picture of that prophet, the working of God within the weakness of a man, that endears our hearts to him. That is the work of restoration. It didn't just happen in a church, it happened in a boy.

I once sat on a picnic bench just outside the Sacred Grove and listened to a man bear testimony of the young boy who had walked into the middle of those trees and prayed. My heart was filled with the truth he witnessed of. At the very end, that humble man said one sentence I will never forget: "Next to Jesus, I love Joseph most."

It is a phrase I have repeated hundreds of times. At the foot of Cumorah. In the midst of the grove. From a window in Carthage.

Praise to the man.

This will be a year of studying questions and answers and stories. We will learn of great heroes and fallen Saints. We will witness mighty miracles and epic failures. Through it all, we will be reminded of the God who oversaw it all—a God who restores and gathers, who embraces weakness and extends grace.

A God who answers the questions of obscure boys of little consequence.

This is the story of a boy named Joseph, and the building of a kingdom, and the gathering up of The Church of Jesus Christ of Latter-day Saints.

It's his story, and your story, and my story.

And it all started with a simple prayer in a grove of trees, and a God who answers. —EBF

JOSEPH SMITH—HISTORY 1:15

I kneeled down and began to
offer up the desires of my heart to God.

I recently visited with a Hindu priest who asked me a simple question: "What do you want?" He then told me something very wise (which you would expect from a Hindu priest, right?). He said, "That is an easy question to give an answer to, but a difficult question to give a *good* answer to." He was so very correct. What *did* I want? At that moment, Taco Bell. But what about life? What do I want? As Joseph Smith did, I reflected on this question again and again—what is it that I actually, really want? Joseph wanted salvation. He was worried about the state of his soul and the fate of mankind. That was what took him to the revival meetings and the church services. That was what took him to the book of James. That was what took him to the grove of trees near his house.

There seems to be something preparatory about the reflecting and desiring in Joseph's story. He didn't close the Bible after reading James 1:5 and walk right into the woods. There was a period of wondering, seeking, thinking, and pondering. Perhaps—just maybe—those were the actions that carved out a place in his mind and heart for the answer that he would receive. To truly desire something has a significant impact on our soul—especially if what we are desiring has a direct connection with our soul.

It has always been significant to me that one of the first things Joseph learned in the grove was that he was forgiven of his sins. Of all the questions and answers that happened in that First Vision encounter, it seems to me as if the first might have been in response to what he desired most of all. —DB

Reflect and Respond

What do you want right now? What do you actually desire most?

Your favorite
scripture in Joseph
Smith—History 1

DOCTRINE AND COVENANTS 1:1

Hearken

The first section of the Doctrine and Covenants is often called the preface. Have you ever wondered who wrote the first section, why it was written, or when it was written? The answer can be found in D&C 1:6, "Behold, this is mine authority, and the authority of my servants, and *my* preface unto the book of my commandments, which I have given them to publish unto you" (emphasis added). This section was actually not the first revelation Joseph received. It came after an attempt from Sidney Rigdon, Oliver Cowdery, and William E. McLellin to write a preface to the Book of Commandments, but none seemed right, so Joseph petitioned the Lord to ask what to do. The Lord wrote His own preface instead.[2]

An entire lesson could be devoted to the first word the Lord used in His preface. *Hearken* can mean "to hear with attention and obedience, to listen carefully or to consider diligently." When written in Japanese characters, the word is depicted with symbols meaning *ear, you, eyes, hear,* and *undivided attention.* The word *hearken* is found more than 230 times in the Bible and almost that many times in modern scripture.

The preface of this book begins with an invitation to enter in, to consider diligently, and to listen carefully with undivided attention and obedience. It is an invitation that is going to require something of you. The Lord doesn't just want your ears, He wants the whole of you. His preface is filled with counsel and warning, prophecies and promises. It contains His words to those who were at the special conference, but also to all who begin a study of this book. "*Hearken, . . . the voice of the Lord is unto all*" (D&C 1:1–2; emphasis added).

This is a book that was written for you. —EBF

Reflect and Respond

As you read through section 1, look specifically for the counsel, warnings, prophecies, and promises. Consider writing them down.

Your favorite scripture in
Section 1

DOCTRINE AND COVENANTS 2:2

The promises made to the fathers...

In a baseball lineup, you put one of your strongest batters first. That person is sometimes called the "leadoff hitter." As the earliest section, as far as dates go, for the whole Doctrine and Covenants, section 2 becomes the leadoff message for the book. It was written after the first of Joseph Smith's many encounters with an angel. Joseph's prayer was for forgiveness of his sins. In answer, the angel Moroni came with a message. Moroni stayed through the night, giving instruction and quoting ancient scripture. One of those scriptures came from Malachi—the last of the Hebrew prophets in ancient times. The words, in fact, are the last recorded words of the Old Testament—a book that ends on a cliff-hanger, with a promise waiting to be fulfilled.

More than 2200 years had passed between the time that Malachi spoke his prophecy and the night that Moroni quoted it to Joseph. Some might be tempted to think that God had forgotten those promises made so long ago. But Moroni came with a different message: a message put at the beginning of the Doctrine and Covenants to remind Joseph and all those who read those words that God intends to fulfill all of His promises, even if it takes 2200 years. He is a God who is both willing and able to do what He has said He will do. He remembers His promises to the fathers.

His personal visit to Joseph in the grove and then His subsequent visits through angels and other means are a constant reminder through Restoration scripture that God has not forgotten His people. —DB

Reflect and Respond

What promises of God are you holding onto right now? What is giving you hope and trust to keep holding onto them?

Your favorite scripture in Section 2

DOCTRINE AND COVENANTS 3:9-10

Behold, thou art Joseph, and thou wast chosen to do the
work of the Lord, . . . **and thou art still chosen.**

It was after the 116 pages had been lost, after his first son had died, after he had cared for Emma during her recovery from the trauma of childbirth and of loss, after the Urim and Thummim had been taken in consequence of his constant wearying of the Lord, that Joseph went for a walk. There, a heavenly messenger met him and finally gave Joseph the opportunity to inquire of the Lord again through the Urim and Thummim.

Have you ever wondered how that conversation might have gone? Well, section 3 contains those words. When you read this section, perhaps what you will notice first is the rebuke and the command to repent, but there is a far greater lesson here. When you make a mistake, the Lord doesn't just tell you what you did wrong, He reminds you who you are. "Behold, thou art Joseph, and thou wast chosen to do the work of the Lord" (D&C 3:9). And then, just in case Joseph didn't listen the first time, the Lord repeated it again, " . . . thou art still chosen, and art again called to the work" (D&C 3:10).

Has that ever been true in your life? Often, when we make a mistake, all we see is the mistake. We *become* the mistake, and our heart drags, and our thoughts fill up with failure. Sometimes it's hard to move past the mistake. In those moments, it would be wise to remember the Lord's message to Joseph: *I saw the mistake. Repent. Move past it. I know who you are, you are still chosen, and I have a work for you to do.*

Righting the wrong is important, but remembering who God sees in you in that moment is just as important. He knows each of us will make mistakes. He has planned for mistakes. What He doesn't want is for us to lose sight of His future plans for us. —EBF

Reflect and Respond

Consider a time when the memory of who you are in God's eyes has helped you to move past a mistake. What did you learn?

Your favorite
scripture in
Section 3

DOCTRINE AND COVENANTS 4:3

If ye have desires to serve God ye are called to the work.

For years, Joseph Smith Sr., the Prophet's father, had kept himself distant from organized religion and the churches near his home. But the Restoration sparked something different in him. He was an avid and zealous supporter of the work. Section 4 came during difficult days. Joseph had not translated much of the Book of Mormon (if any) in the previous six months, since the whole episode with the loss of the 116 pages. Perhaps there was a lot of confusion, mourning, and discouragement resting on young Joseph's heart. Father Smith came down to Harmony, Pennsylvania, where Joseph was then living, with one question: How can I help?

Sometimes I wonder if the visit and the asking of the question didn't breathe new life into the Prophet. Ever since Joseph's visit from Moroni, his father had encouraged him to go and do what God wanted him to do. Father Smith came asking how to help in the work when in reality he already was helping—perhaps without even knowing it.

Of all the words Father Smith heard from the Lord, some of my favorite ones are the Lord's simple invitation: "If ye have desires . . . ye are called." In other words, if you want to be a part of this great work, then I will let you. It doesn't take much to make a significant impact, and it doesn't take much to get going. Just desire and a willing heart. The Lord's invitation was so welcoming that even a fifty-eight-year-old farmer who might not have attended church very often during the years before Joseph's vision was welcome and encouraged to play a part. He entered into the work immediately, and his enthusiasm led others to ask the same question: How can I help?

How can you? —DB

Reflect and Respond

In what simple and significant ways can you move God's work forward, which always involves lifting and loving people?

Your favorite scripture in Section 4

DOCTRINE AND COVENANTS 5:23

And now, again, I speak unto you, my servant Joseph,
concerning the man that desires the witness.

Some believe that Joseph had not seen Martin Harris for almost eight months when the revelation in section 5 was given.[3] The last time Martin had been mentioned in the scriptures was when Joseph was being rebuked by God, "And when thou deliveredst up that which God had given thee sight and power to translate, thou deliveredst up that which was sacred into the hands of a wicked man" (D&C 3:12). How many of us would want to be recognized by God with the title of *wicked*?

From that verse, you might have thought that the Lord had given up on Martin, or maybe that Joseph would have. Surely the experience of losing the pages would have left a bad taste in his mouth. But when Martin traveled to Harmony, Pennsylvania, that March to ask Joseph for a witness of the gold plates, Joseph petitioned the Lord. Through revelation, Joseph was told that there would be three witnesses of the gold plates, and that Martin Harris would be one.

It wasn't until three months later, sometime in June 1829, that Martin Harris finally received that witness. What is remarkable is that he did. Joseph did not give up on Martin, and neither did the Lord. Martin Harris transformed from a wicked man to a witness almost one year to the date of his altercation with the Lord and Joseph.

This section reminds us not only that ours is a God of second chances but also that God will allow wicked men to become witnesses if they are humble in mighty prayer and faith and if their hearts are sincere.

It is the promise of His grace.

It is His work and His glory. —EBF

Reflect and Respond

What does this story teach you about second chances? How does that make you feel?

Your favorite scripture in
Section 5

DOCTRINE AND COVENANTS 6:22

Cast your mind upon the night
that you cried unto me in your heart.

We each have moments in life when we are awakened to just how aware God is of us. I have started calling these "Oliver moments." The work of translating the Book of Mormon was puttering along slowly in the early spring of 1829—that is, until the Lord orchestrated the friendship between Joseph Smith and Oliver Cowdery. Oliver's brother, Warren, was scheduled to board at the Smith home as a teacher but was unable to fulfill the assignment. Oliver took his place.

It didn't take long living in the Smith house before Oliver knew that something magnificent was happening there behind the scenes. It's hard to keep gold plates a secret. After pressing about it, Oliver finally learned from the family about the work Joseph had been called to do. Soon he was on his way, and, two days after arriving in Harmony, Oliver started scribing full time for Joseph.

Oliver hadn't been there for many days before Joseph received a revelation for him. In it we find out that, unbeknownst to Joseph, Oliver had spent some nights wondering in prayer if the work he was so fully engaged in really was God's work. I am curious to know what feelings swelled in Oliver's heart when he heard those words in the revelation, to "cast [his] mind upon the night that [he] cried" to the Lord. That was a prayer that only Oliver and God knew about. In that moment, Oliver received a witness not only that the translation was of God but, perhaps more powerfully, that God knew him, the details of his life, and the wonderings of his heart. —DB

Reflect and Respond

When have you had an "Oliver moment," a moment when you knew that God knew you?

Your favorite scripture in
Section 6

DOCTRINE AND COVENANTS 7:5

. . . this was a good desire; but my beloved has desired that he might do more,
or **a greater work . . . than what he has before done.**

It was in April 1829 that Joseph Smith and Oliver Cowdery asked the Lord whether "John, the beloved disciple, tarried in the flesh or had died" (D&C 7, section heading). The answer was translated from "parchment written and hid up by John the beloved,"[4] which is why this section begins in the first person with the Apostle John speaking. Before we consider the lesson of this conversation, it might be interesting to compare a similar conversation recorded in John 21:21–24. Take a few minutes to read those verses. What do you learn from this section that might help you understand John 21 a little better?

At first glance, after reading this section, you might think that the Lord is saying that John is doing a greater work than Peter, which doesn't sound like what we know of the Lord. If we read the entire phrase, we realize that John has asked to do "*a greater work . . . than what he has before done*" (D&C 7:5; emphasis added). This teaches an important lesson. The Lord does not want us to measure our work or our worth compared with someone else's. He wants us to measure it against the measure He gives each of us for ourselves. John wanted to do more than what *he* had done before. He wasn't finished. He felt there was a greater work for him to do.

This section reminds us that Peter's choice was not wrong just because it was different from John's. The Lord's response to these two different choices is so insightful: "Verily I say unto you, ye shall both have according to your desires, for ye both joy in that which ye have desired" (D&C 7:8). —EBF

Reflect and Respond

When have you desired something different from someone else and afterward realized that both were good choices?

Your favorite
scripture in
Section 7

DOCTRINE AND COVENANTS 8:4

This is thy gift . . .

Every other day, walking to class, I would pass a poster that hung in one of the hallways at BYU. Every time I would walk past, that same poster would catch my eye. It was a picture of a man teaching in a classroom, with a phrase printed across the top that asked, "Do you want to teach the youth of the Church?" Usually when I walked that hallway, I would glance at it out of the corner of my eye—as if I were worried that the poster would notice that I had interest. I pretended I didn't, because I didn't want to be a teacher. But the poster called to me. One day, after I passed it, I finally let out a sigh and did an about-face to return to look at it and get the details. As I stared at it, a sense of intrigue settled on me, and I remembered a line from my patriarchal blessing about teaching. It was as if the Lord were whispering to me, "This is thy gift . . ."

That is the line that God whispered to Oliver during the translation of the Book of Mormon—a time when he discovered some of his own spiritual gifts. We don't know much about what led him to wonder and ask, but sometime in the midst of the translation work, his intrigue led to the Lord teaching him what some of his gifts were and encouraging him to pursue them and use them to fill the world with more good. All throughout scripture, God encourages His people to pursue and discover the gifts He has given us. He is anxious for us to learn what they are and how to use them.

Listen for the moments when He might whisper that same phrase to you: "*This* is thy gift . . ." —DB

Reflect and Respond

What spiritual gifts have you discovered in yourself? How did the Lord lead you to discovering them?

Your favorite scripture in Section 8

DOCTRINE AND COVENANTS 9:7

You took no thought save it was to ask me.

I remember once receiving a calling I felt unqualified for—I wasn't sure I had the talents, the time, or the wisdom. Just after the bishop left our house, I remember kneeling down and complaining to the Lord, *"Why me? Why now?"* The next day I woke up feeling overwhelmed and decided to drive to the temple. It had been twelve hours, and, resigned to my fate, I now had a different question for the Lord: "What do you want me to do?" When I arrived at the temple, the line for initiatory work was long enough that I had time to read the scriptures while I waited. I turned to D&C 9 and read this verse, "Behold, you have not understood; you have supposed that I would give it unto you, when you took no thought save it was to ask me." It was as if the Lord were speaking right to me. I spent the next few minutes asking those first two questions again, but this time my request was humble and genuine, I really wanted to know, "Why me? Why now?" What talents did I have that were crucial for that calling right now? What unique gifts could I bring into my service?

Oliver Cowdery faced a similar situation. The Lord had given Oliver the gift to translate, but in this section we learn why that opportunity was removed. First, he didn't put forth the effort required to make use of the gift or take the time to understand it. *He took no thought save it was to ask.* Second, he feared. The fear prevented Oliver from using his gift.

Oliver teaches us the importance of accepting God's call and then having the courage to move forward into that capacity even if we feel inadequate. It requires us to study, ask, and feel. The Lord doesn't intend to give us all the answers immediately. There is growth that comes from engaging and obtaining an understanding for ourselves. —EBF

Reflect and Respond

What has the Lord called you to do? Take some time to sincerely ask those two questions: Why me? Why now?

Your favorite scripture in
Section 9

DOCTRINE AND COVENANTS 10:43

My wisdom is greater than the cunning of the devil.

We can't fault Martin Harris for pressuring Joseph to allow him to take some of the translated pages of the Book of Mormon as proof of the project to his wife and other family members. He had sacrificed time, money, and his good name to help in a work that everyone else considered bogus. We could also never blame Joseph for trusting Martin with those pages even after the Lord said no. Martin was one of Joseph's only supporters outside his own family and was several years older and more experienced than Joseph was.

However, as we know, the pages were lost, and enemies had orchestrated a plan to change them so that when the book was published, it would be proven a fake. I cannot even imagine the sinking feeling in Joseph's gut and soul. The Lord had told him not to give Martin the pages, and Joseph had persisted. Joseph thought he had ruined the work, and so did those who stole the pages. What none of them knew was that, more than 2300 years before this ever happened, the Lord, who already knew it would happen, had also already orchestrated the solution. Through the efforts of two ancient prophets who followed commandments they didn't fully understand, the plates included additional records to replace the pages that would be lost.

I wish I could have seen the faces of those who were intent on destroying the work when they first read the finished manuscript. We cannot make a mistake that the Lord cannot fix, repair, or weave into the pattern of our lives. His wisdom is greater. There is no trick of the devil He doesn't already know and (in many cases) hasn't already created solutions for. We can trust in Him. —DB

Reflect and Respond

What perspective does this account give you about your own mistakes? How have you seen evidence of God's ultimate wisdom?

Your favorite scripture in Section 10

DOCTRINE AND COVENANTS 11:12

Put your trust in that Spirit
which leadeth to do good.

It has been my opportunity to teach youth all over the United States. On many occasions I am asked to participate in Q&A sessions with these youth. The most common question I get asked is, "How do I know if it is the Spirit talking to me?" Section 11 is my favorite place to find the answer to that question. In this section the Lord gives Hyrum six ways to recognize the Spirit:

- It leads you to do good.
- It leads you to do justly.
- It leads you to walk humbly.
- It leads you to judge righteously.
- It will enlighten your mind.
- It will fill your soul with joy.

I tell the youth that we won't always know if it is the Spirit speaking to us, but section 11 gives us some good guidelines to refer to if we are wondering. If you feel prompted to do something good, you can trust it is the Spirit. If you feel inspired to choose right over wrong, most likely the Spirit. If you are filled with humility or you are led to discover the good in someone, there's a good chance it's the Spirit. In those moments when your mind fills with inspiration that isn't your own, or when you feel an increase of joy, you are most likely feeling the Spirit. Every time I read that list, I realize that the Spirit is playing a larger role in my life than I often realize. It is a gift for which I am intensely grateful. —EBF

Reflect and Respond

Look through the list above and consider how many of those definitions of the Spirit you have experienced this week.

Your favorite scripture in
Section 11

DOCTRINE AND COVENANTS 12:8

. . . whatsoever shall be entrusted to his care.

Joseph Knight was one of the first people to help provide Joseph and Emma with necessities. Loyal from the very beginning, he was influential in the couple's courtship and sacrificed his own goods to help care for them. He and his family remained faithful to Joseph throughout his life.

In May 1829, Joseph Knight "was very anxious to know his duty regarding this work."[5] The Lord told Father Knight, "No one can assist in this work except he shall be humble and full of love, having faith, hope, and charity, being temperate in all things, whatsoever shall be entrusted to his care" (D&C 12:8).

Father Knight took that counsel to heart. He was full of love, but there was more. In the midst of turmoil, Joseph and Emma found a friend in Father Knight—a friend who would stand beside them, add to their efforts to build God's kingdom, and welcome them into his home and his heart. His rule of life was love, and he lived it by being careful with all the things that had been entrusted into his care, including Joseph and Emma. It was a time of unrest, a time when many were questioning Joseph. The persecution that would follow Joseph and Emma for the rest of their lives had just begun in earnest. And yet, Father Knight was a friend to them in a time when Joseph and Emma were desperate for friends.

Now, hundreds of years later, I hear what people say about the Prophet of the Restoration. How they disregard his words. How they distance themselves. Just like during the falling away that happened in the time of the Knight family, I hear the accusations, the discontent, the doubt—and I make a commitment to myself.

For all the days of my life, I want to be known as a friend to Joseph. —EBF

Reflect and Respond

What is one thing you could learn from Father Knight about the things that have been entrusted into your care?

Your favorite scripture in Section 12

DOCTRINE AND COVENANTS 13:1

Fellow servants . . .

While translating the Book of Mormon, Joseph and Oliver came across the Savior's words to the Nephites about baptism in Third Nephi. I imagine the thought of baptism both intrigued them and thrilled them. At some point, that wonder prompted them to ask if that same gift of baptism could also be theirs. In the familiar pattern Joseph had adopted of turning to the Lord whenever he had a question, the two of them went to the banks of the nearby river to ask. In answer to their prayer, the great prophet John the Baptist appeared to them and gave them gifts, powers, and keys—perhaps more than they were expecting. That seems to be one of the Lord's patterns: to give more than we ask. Could the miracles get any more spectacular? The man who stood in the River Jordan with Jesus, who had sacrificed his life for truth, was now instructing them and placing his hands on each of their heads, bestowing power and keys upon them—including the ministering of angels. In a way, they were being called to the work and ministry of angels by an angel—called to the work of bestowing truth and gifts upon others.

I have often wondered if their hearts surged when they heard the great John the Baptist use the phrase "Upon you my fellow servants." *Fellow servants.* He considered them equals and companions in the great work of the gospel. It was a different river, at a different time, and their commission was different in the details, but in reality they had the same mission as John: the giving of gifts and the introducing of Jesus to others. —DB

Reflect and Respond

Who has been an angel in your life and brought gifts and goodness and Jesus to you? How can you bring those gifts to others?

Your favorite scripture in
Section 13

DOCTRINE AND COVENANTS 14:11

And behold, thou art David,
and **thou art called to assist . . .**

David Whitmer was one of the first members of the Church baptized in this dispensation and one of the Three Witnesses of the Book of Mormon. He was present for most of the important beginning stages of the Church. Section 14 was written in answer to David's earnest question about his individual duty in the Church. Within the revelation one verse stands out: "Thou art David, and thou art called to assist" (D&C 14:11). Every time I read that word *assist,* I wonder what David thought. Was he disappointed? Or was he eager to begin?

Here is something worth noting. It is interesting that their role to assist was so important that, thousands of years before the Church was restored, the Lord told Moroni about David Whitmer and Oliver Cowdery. He described them like this: "And behold, ye may be privileged that ye may show the plates unto those who shall *assist* to bring forth this work; and unto three shall they be shown" (Ether 5:2–3; emphasis added). Thousands of years before, the Lord knew David would be one of those called to assist with the great work that would come forth. That is remarkable to me.

Sadly, the Lord followed up his assignment to David with this phrase, "which thing *if ye do, and are faithful . . .*" (D&C 14:11; emphasis added). Not only did the Lord give David an assignment, He gave him a warning. The failure to heed that warning would eventually remove David's opportunity to assist. In later years he would leave the Church, but he would never renounce his witness of the Book of Mormon. —EBF

Reflect and Respond

How have you been called to assist in bringing forth the fulness of the gospel today? How can you be faithful to that work?

Your favorite
scripture in
Section 14

DOCTRINE AND COVENANTS 15–16

Intimately and impressively personal

The Whitmer family became loyal and zealous supporters and defenders of Joseph Smith and the work of the Restoration right from the beginning. Together with their brother David, Peter and John came to Joseph looking for instructions and direction in what they could do to help, or assist, in the work they had become enamored with. The two brothers were seven years apart in age (John was twenty-seven and Peter was twenty), with different vocational paths and gifts, but the Lord gave them both the same counsel: "The thing which will be of the most worth unto you will be to declare repentance unto this people, that you may bring souls unto me" (D&C 15:6; 16:6). In fact, that was not the only line that was the same from the two separate revelations. Except for the names of John and Peter, the two revelations are identical, word for word. This has always made me chuckle and wonder a little when I read the heading to section 15, which says, "The message is intimately and impressively personal." At first glance, it doesn't seem very intimate or personal at all, with the next section being just the same, basically a copy and paste.

And then I think about my own call to serve. Except for a name and a date and a place, it was identical to the missionary calls of every one of my friends who received their letters that same winter. Every word. And yet, as I read it, it felt very intimate, and my experiences were impressively personal. It was from the Lord to me—just me.

So many moments are like this. Same talks, prayers, hymns, and words in ordinances—and yet we walk away from those moments with personal inspiration and experiences and impressions and the knowledge that the Lord will speak just to us in a personal and intimate way. —DB

Reflect and Respond

When have you read a scripture or heard a talk or sung a hymn with others and had an intimate and impressively personal experience?

Your favorite scripture in Sections 15–16

DOCTRINE AND COVENANTS 17:8

The gates of hell **shall not prevail against you.**

When my son flew to Croatia to serve his mission, he had a long layover in Paris. He was traveling completely alone to his mission, so I asked him to call me and check in once he had found his gate. He was supposed to call at four a.m., but the minutes kept ticking by without a phone call. I started to panic. When the phone finally rang, I asked, "What took you so long?" before even saying hello.

"Mom, you are not going to believe this," he replied, laughing. "I went to check the gate and make sure I knew where I was, but I was super early for the flight, so no one was in the whole hallway. When I tried to walk back to where the phones were, someone had shut the gate and locked that part of the terminal down with me inside!"

"Oh, dear!" I said. "What did you do?"

"I waited for a cleaning lady to come by, and then I pointed to the lock and told her the only French word I know, *Merci,* and she let me out."

Can you imagine being locked behind a gate you can't get out of?

In section 17, the three men who were about to become witnesses to the Book of Mormon received a beautiful promise from the Lord. If they would keep the last commandments that the Lord had given, "the gates of hell shall not prevail against you" (D&C 17:8). The promise was clear: if they testified of the truth, they would not be locked in.

Although each of these men left the Church at some point, none of them ever denied his testimony of the Book of Mormon. —EBF

Reflect and Respond
Write down or share your witness of the Book of Mormon with someone today.

Your favorite scripture in
Section 17

DOCTRINE AND COVENANTS 18:10

The worth of souls is great in the sight of God.

My kids are so interested in what things cost these days. They ask about everything. How much is that? What did you pay for this? How long would it take me to earn that? I am not sure where it comes from, but it seems to be a human thing—to wonder about cost and worth. Sometimes when they ask me what something costs, I don't give a number. Instead I say, "It depends on what you would pay. That is the definition of worth: what someone is willing to give up or pay for something else."

This revelation in the Doctrine and Covenants was originally directed to David Whitmer and Oliver Cowdery, but it also included instructions to a future audience— the Quorum of the Twelve Apostles. David and Oliver would eventually be given the responsibility to choose the original members of the quorum. Each of them was given a similar commission and instruction for the work they were being called to do—a work that centered on the souls of mankind. In the instruction, the Lord taught them about the worth of these souls. To God, their worth was great. Why? Because "the Lord your Redeemer suffered death . . . suffered the pain of all men" for them (D&C 18:11). That was the cost. Worth is what someone is willing to pay, and the Lord was willing to give His whole life for you. That is why your worth is great in His eyes.

Of everything that Oliver, David, and the Twelve would need to know when they went out to teach and interact with people, it seems like this is what the Lord wanted them to know first. In the work of saving souls, it is important to remember that *the worth of every one of them is great in His eyes.* —DB

Reflect and Respond

How does your view of people change when you hear the Lord talk about their worth? How can your thoughts and actions reflect His?

Your favorite scripture in
Section 18

DOCTRINE AND COVENANTS 19:26

I command thee that thou shalt not covet thine
own property, but **impart it freely.**

After a period of searching, Joseph Smith and Martin Harris finally found and agreed upon a printer who could print the Book of Mormon for them—a man named E. B. Grandin. Because they wanted to print 5,000 copies, the cost for all the supplies was too much for Mr. Grandin to risk. He needed a guarantee of payment before he started. From the revelation, it seems that Martin Harris had initially agreed to mortgage his farm and all the property he owned to give the backing, but then had started to waver in his commitment and confidence. If the book didn't sell, Martin would lose everything. He was being asked to give all, and to give it freely, to be liberal in his support of the printing of the Book of Mormon. But what a risk!

Throughout my life, I have met a few people who were liberal in their gifts and would give freely when something was needed. There is a rare kind of person who never shows a hint of hesitation when help is being asked. But most of the people I know, understandably, seem to waver like Martin.

It makes me wonder where the unwavering people got that kind of heart. Perhaps they inherited it from the Lord, who spends the first part of the revelation explaining how freely He gave Himself. Immediately before the command to Martin, He says, "I am Jesus Christ; I came by the will of the Father, and I do his will" (D&C 19:24). He gave His life, His blood, and His heart freely. He was liberal in His goodness. When He asks us to give all—and to give it freely—He asks no more than what He has already done. —DB

Reflect and Respond

Who do you know who has the kind of heart that gives freely?
What things might the Lord be asking you to give freely?

Your favorite
scripture in
Section 19

DOCTRINE AND COVENANTS 20:17

By these things we know . . .

One of my favorite parts of this section is the list of "we know" statements that begins in verse 17 and ends in verse 31.

- We know there is a God in heaven.
- We know that he created man.
- We know he gave unto them commandments.
- We know about the fall of man.
- We know God gave his Only Begotten Son to be crucified.
- We know that as many believe and are baptized in His holy name and endure in faith will be saved.
- We believe in the words of the holy prophets.
- We believe in the Holy Ghost.
- We believe the Father, Son, and Holy Ghost are one God, infinite and eternal, without end.
- We know all men must repent and believe on the name of Jesus Christ.
- We know that justification through the grace of our Lord and Savior is true.
- We know that sanctification through the grace of our Lord and Savior is true.
- We know that these things are true.

Every time I read that list, it makes me want to take a second to write down my own list of "I know" statements. Making a list of what we know can become a powerful witness and anchor in years to come. —EBF

Reflect and Respond
Take some time today to create a list of what you know.

Your favorite
scripture in
Section 20

DOCTRINE AND COVENANTS 21:9

I will bless all those who labor in
my vineyard with **a mighty blessing.**

In a little log cabin in Fayette, New York, on the day the Church of Jesus Christ was reorganized, Oliver Cowdery put his hands upon Joseph Smith's head and ordained him as a prophet, seer, and revelator. It was a position that included the gifts and responsibilities to teach and direct and warn in the name of the Lord. In that setting, in front of all those present, Joseph received a revelation that included promises and blessings to those who heard the Prophet's words and obeyed them as if they were from the Lord. The Lord promised them a mighty blessing: that He would "cause the heavens to shake for your good, and his name's glory" (D&C 21:6).

I love to think about and try to picture such a blessing. What would that look like in my life? Our family once went to Mexico and spent some time at an orphanage. On one of the nights, we did a piñata with the kids. After several unsuccessful batters came through, my brother finally grabbed the piñata and started to shake the candy out. I wish you could have heard the squeals and seen the way the kids ran in. It was so exciting, and their laughter was so infectious, that I found myself—a grown man—on the ground laughing and grabbing at the candy with them.

That is what I picture when the Lord promises the heavens will shake for our good. One of the ways He would show us how to receive these promises is through prophets, seers, and revelators. That would be their job—to show us how heaven will absolutely shake for the good of each of God's children. —DB

Reflect and Respond

Have you seen these mighty blessings in your own life? Has heaven shaken for your good?

Your favorite
scripture in
Section 21

DOCTRINE AND COVENANTS 22:4

Enter ye in . . .

One of the first questions people asked after the organization of the Church was about rebaptism for those who had already been baptized in another church. Did they need to be baptized again to join the Church, or was their previous baptism sufficient? The question was taken to the Lord, and the answer is found in this particular revelation.

When I read the Doctrine and Covenants, it makes me wonder how many questions are still pouring in to Church leaders today for different scenarios and circumstances. Remember that each of these revelations in the past (and today) came in answer to actual questions or concerns or problems from real people facing real situations. I think the Lord likes situations that require asking. They keep His children in constant communication with Him—communication that He adores.

When I was serving as a bishop, there were several times when I would knock on doors of people who would not particularly want to talk to me. I had a lot of front-porch conversations. On other occasions, it was always so refreshing to hear someone say, "Come on in." It made me feel so welcome and appreciated when I heard that. I love the line in this revelation about baptism that has a similar feel: "Enter ye in." The Lord is anxious for us to enter into conversation, enter into His covenant and His kingdom, and eventually enter into His presence. There is always an invitation for us to enter in. We are not just welcome there; we are encouraged to come. We will be missed if we don't. —DB

Reflect and Respond

How do you feel to be so welcomed—just as you are—into conversation and relationship with the Lord?

Your favorite scripture in **Section 22**

DOCTRINE AND COVENANTS 23:3

Thy calling is **to exhortation**,
and **to strengthen** the church continually.

A year before this revelation was given, Hyrum visited Joseph in Harmony, Pennsylvania. At that time, the Lord told him, "Seek not to declare my word, but first seek to obtain my word, and then shall your tongue be loosed . . . yea, the power of God unto the convincing of men. But now hold your peace" (D&C 11:21–22). Have you ever wanted to be a part of something and then been told to wait? I remember a son who tried out for the high school soccer team two years in a row before making the team. A friend who struggled with infertility, and then finally carried and delivered her baby girl. I think of my good friend who is struggling with cancer and currently in the midst of the waiting. After one year of Hyrum's waiting, the Lord finally responded, "Thy heart is opened, and thy tongue loosed; and thy calling is to exhortation, and to strengthen the church continually" (D&C 23:3).

During the very next year, Hyrum had the opportunity to testify as one of the Eight Witnesses of the Book of Mormon. His life was devoted to giving words of encouragement and strength to those in the Church. He would eventually die as a martyr with his brother, sealing his witness with his own blood. His witness still continues to exhort and strengthen the Church.

Have you ever wondered what the Lord is preparing you for? Perhaps you are in a waiting place. Maybe this is a time for you to hold your peace. In the quiet moments, seek to obtain His word and His direction. The Lord has something in store for you. Hyrum reminds us that callings of exhortation and strength are often preceded by moments of waiting and holding our peace. —EBF

Reflect and Respond

Are you in a moment of waiting and holding your peace, or a moment of exhortation and strengthening the Church?

Your favorite
scripture in
Section 23

DOCTRINE AND COVENANTS 24:12

And I will give unto him **strength**
such as is not known among men.

I remember being shocked when I started my mission because it was so difficult. Wasn't the Lord supposed to open the way? Many years after that, I remember expecting my life to get a little better and easier when I received a busier calling in my ward. Wasn't that part of the package deal? Service equals blessings?

Perhaps Joseph and Oliver had similar thoughts in the weeks and months following the publication of the Book of Mormon and the organization of the Church. Why was the persecution increasing? Things were so bad that there were several people, including Emma, who were unable to be confirmed after their baptisms because of mobs and false accusations. Joseph was arrested and stood trial at least twice during those days. I always have to remind myself how young Joseph and Oliver were at the time. They were twenty-four and twenty-three years old, trying to run and direct the kingdom of God on the earth with so little experience and a heap of backlash from neighbors. Perhaps they had the same kind of thoughts as I did when I began my service. *If this is God's work, why isn't He shielding us from some of this? Where are His blessings?*

Some of the answers to these questions came in these sections, but one of my favorites is the advice the Lord wanted Joseph to give Oliver. The Lord said to tell him, "I will give unto him strength such as is not known among men" (D&C 24:12). I love hearing the Lord essentially say, "I will not shield you from this, but I will strengthen you through it. It will be a kind of strength you haven't seen on the earth yet." It might have been scary for Oliver to know he would need it, but awe-inspiring to know he would have it. —DB

Reflect and Respond

When have you felt this kind of strength? Have you felt the surge of God's power as you faced problems bigger than you?

Your favorite
scripture in
Section 24

DOCTRINE AND COVENANTS 25:3

Thou art an elect lady, whom I have called.

Whenever I read "Emma's chapter," section 25 of the Doctrine and Covenants, I am fascinated with the words *daughter, faithful, virtue, elect, office, meekness, ordained, cleave, covenants,* and *crown.* They are words that speak to me of royalty, of great importance, and of high calling. I love that the Lord spoke those words to Emma.

Every time I read section 25, I also read Proverbs 31. Some people call verses 10–31 of Proverbs 31 *Eshet Chayil,* which means "woman of valor." In some Jewish homes, these verses are read or sung to the mother in the home on Friday evening. I love this thought of tribute to the mother, spoken almost as a prayer, on the eve of the Sabbath, just after the Sabbath candles have been lit. It is a reminder of who she is and who she can become. To me, it whispers of the majesty of women.

Section 25 hints of this *Eshet Chayil.* Emma is to be ordained to expound scriptures and to exhort the Church. She will comfort her husband. She will write and learn. Section 25 helps us to understand that the Lord was not planning on Emma's being a silent partner in the Restoration. She was meant to help lead it. This section reminds us how the Lord views His daughters and the great work He has in store for each of them. And this was not just Emma's calling. The last verse of this section contains an important piece of counsel, "this is my voice unto all" (D&C 25:16). Exhort the Church. Live up to the office of your calling. Expound scripture. Thou art an elect lady, a woman of valor. God needs your voice and your gifts and your wisdom to further His work.

There is a place for you. —EBF

Reflect and Respond

Where else in scripture do you recognize the importance and worth of women in God's eyes? What do you learn from their stories?

Your favorite scripture in Section 25

DOCTRINE AND COVENANTS 26:1

Let your time be devoted to the studying . . . until after you
shall go . . . and then it shall be made known what you shall do.

My friend texted me recently asking how things were going. Usually I respond to such questions with a "Hey, man! Super good! You?" But this is the type of friend to whom I can tell the truth. You know those? So I told him how heavy my load is right now. They're all good things, but my life and schedule are absolutely filled to the brim and spilling over. And then the shower broke and wouldn't turn off. I closed my eyes and just said, "I can't." Every single thing going on is something I signed up for and something I like, but the weight of it all still has been consuming me.

A good friend recently told me that she takes a day each week (in addition to the Sabbath) to say no to all the things—even the good ones. A day to be recharged and to plan and to think and to enjoy—all things the soul needs desperately. A day set apart. A consecrated day. A devoted time.

I love the Lord's very similar advice to Joseph, Oliver, and John Whitmer in July 1830. Ever since Joseph had received the plates in 1827, his life had been complicated and overwhelming. There was no rest between the translations, the organization of the Church, the confirmations, the arrests, the mobs, family responsibilities—everything! I love that the Lord essentially pulled Joseph aside and told him what he needed to be devoting time to in this particular season of his life. There would be more of all the business later—more revelations, more commands, more persecution—but for that time he needed to be devoted to a few spiritual and practical practices to get rested and be ready for what was to come. Just study. That's it. It thrills me that the Lord knows what is most important in the different seasons of our lives. —DB

Reflect and Respond

What has the Lord directed you to devote your time to during this particular season of life? What blessings are coming from it?

Your favorite
scripture in
Section 26

DOCTRINE AND COVENANTS 27:15

Take upon you my whole armor.

When I read section 27, I can't help but ask, Why did the Lord include a lesson on taking upon us the whole armor of God in a section devoted to understanding the administration of the sacrament? Could there be a lesson there, one that should be pondered? Through the description of the armor of God, it is clear that the Lord is promising spiritual protection. Is the same true of the sacrament? The Apostles teach us that the spiritual protection of the armor of God is individual to the needs of every person, and crafting an armor of protection can be done within the home and at church. "In church we can learn how to assemble and fit [the armor] together. But the actual making of and fitting on of the shield of faith belongs in the family circle. No two can be exactly alike. Each must be handcrafted to individual specifications. This shield of faith is not manufactured on an assembly line, only handmade in a cottage industry."[6]

"Examine your armor. Is there an unguarded or unprotected place? Determine now to add whatever part is missing."[7]

How will you strengthen your armor? Could it be possible that taking the sacrament helps us to strengthen, craft, and mold God's armor? Is the sacrament a means of protection? As you consider these things, it is important to remember that this is not the only place in scripture that teaches about the armor of God. Ephesians 6:11–17 also describes this armor. Take some time today to ponder the verses in both Ephesians 6 and D&C 27. What is similar within the accounts? What is different? What do you learn about the protection of the Lord? —EBF

Reflect and Respond
Read D&C 27:15 and Ephesians 6:11–17. How does studying both help you to understand the armor of God better?

Your favorite scripture in Section 27

DOCTRINE AND COVENANTS 28:8

Thou shalt have revelations . . .

Hiram Page was a respected member of the core leadership of the Church. He was married to one of the Whitmer daughters, brother-in-law to Oliver Cowdery, and one of the Eight Witnesses to the Book of Mormon. He was not an obscure person; he was involved. So when he started telling people that he was receiving revelations from a seer stone, people believed him. Even prominent people like Oliver. And why wouldn't they? That was how Joseph had received several revelations. It took a lot of convincing and heart-to-heart conversations to convince Hiram and others who believed him that the revelations he was receiving were deceptions. Every time I read in the revelation that the Lord wanted Hiram to know that "Satan deceiveth him" (D&C 28:11), I cringe a little. Was he embarrassed? Confused? What about the others?

This is the revelation in which the Lord taught that small group back then and the big group of Church members today that it is the prophet, seer, and revelator (today we call him the President of the Church) who receives revelation for the entire Church. It established the pattern. The role of the prophet is to receive revelation for the whole Church. But I have always loved the fact that, once everything was straightened out, the Lord told Hiram, "thou shalt have revelations." I love the expectation and anticipation in that line. No, he wouldn't receive revelation for the Church, but, yes, *yes,* he would receive personal revelation in the other areas of his life. Yes, he would teach with power. Yes, he would receive direction from heaven—just not for the whole Church. I love how gentle the Lord is in teaching the pattern and how encouraging He is with Hiram and all of us in reminding us to expect revelation. —DB

Reflect and Respond

When was the last time you received direction and revelation from heaven?

Your favorite scripture in Section 28

DOCTRINE AND COVENANTS 29:5

It is his good will to give you the kingdom.

It had been a hard year. I was down in bed with a complicated pregnancy, Greg was struggling at work, and on one particular day, Josh had broken a bone in his arm—and there was nothing I could do about any of it. As Josh sat on the couch next to me waiting for someone to come and take him to the hospital, he pointed to a wooden block on the table in front of us with the words *all is well* printed on the front. "Why did you buy that dumb sign, Mom?" he asked. "All is *not* well." He was right. All was not well.

It was at that time that I stumbled upon this scripture: "Lift up your hearts and be glad, for I am in your midst, and am your advocate with the Father; and it is his good will to give you the kingdom" (D&C 29:5). I was reminded that the Lord was with us, He would advocate for us, and God had good things ahead. This scripture carried us through that dark time, and after a season of hardship, we did arrive at the good things.

I learned two important lessons from that experience. First, the Lord promised to be in our midst, so I looked for Him every single day of that hard season. Second, this was the first time I had ever realized that the Lord's will can be good. I don't know why, but at that time I felt turning something over to the will of God meant things weren't going to turn out. It was a "giving up" phrase in my mind. I had never realized that turning something over to the will of God could actually turn out to be good. That perspective changed my life. It taught me to start praying for God's good will in my life, and then to trust that, no matter what happens or what life looks like, it will be good.

All is well. —EBF

Reflect and Respond

Write about a time when you have experienced God's good will in your life. What did you learn from that experience?

Your favorite scripture in
Section 29

DOCTRINE AND COVENANTS 30:6

Be you afflicted in all his afflictions.

Originally, this section was three separate revelations that included assignments to three different people given during the second conference of the Church of Christ, but these assignments were later put together into one section in the 1835 version of the Doctrine and Covenants (see D&C 30, section heading). It is interesting to me to see side by side these three specific assignments to different places with different counsel. David was being asked to stay home near Fayette and serve, while Peter was being called to a bit more difficult and exotic mission. I wonder every time I read this if a similar culture existed back then as it does today with certain calls. Some seem to be a little more exciting than others. No matter what the differences would be, one thing would be the same—they were all being called to minister to and love people. I particularly love some of the advice given to Peter about Oliver Cowdery, his soon-to-be companion: "Be you afflicted in all his afflictions" (D&C 30:6). There is so much Christlike compassion in that counsel.

When I was a new missionary, I struggled to feel worthy of the call. I felt inadequate and overwhelmed. How could I represent the Savior? He was so good and I was so not. A counselor in the branch presidency gave me advice that was life-changing. He said, "Make other people's problems your problems. Then you don't have time to think of your own." He was teaching me the same lesson as Peter, to be afflicted where others are afflicted. Mourn with those that mourn. What he was really asking me to do was to love and care in the way Jesus would, to follow the example of a God who was willing to take upon Himself the afflictions of us all. That is what representatives of Him would surely do—no matter where they are called to serve. —DB

Reflect and Respond

Who do you know who has exemplified the trait of feeling afflicted when others are afflicted? What have you learned from them?

Your favorite scripture in Section 30

DOCTRINE AND COVENANTS 31:4

You shall begin to preach from this time forth.

When our son Josh was set apart for his mission, he was blessed with good health that would allow him to work every single day of his mission.

I won't forget the email we received one Monday morning that started with this line: "I got hit by a car this week." An ambulance and fire truck were called to the scene. The handlebar of his bike ripped through his shirt, causing a wound in his stomach. He still has that scar. He told us how his knee had been injured.

Then he told us about his new companion, who had been out for only one day. Josh didn't want to ruin the first day of that boy's mission. He declined the ride to the hospital in the ambulance and instead went back to his apartment, changed his bloody shirt, prayed that the Lord would take the pain out of his knee, and then got on his bike and started to ride again. At the end of the letter, Josh told us that what got him through the day was holding onto the line from his setting apart that promised he would be healthy enough to work every day of his mission.

What I love most about section 31 is that it reads like a setting apart. It is a blessing for a man who was about to become a missionary, a man who had been a member of the Church for only one month and had read only sixteen pages of the Book of Mormon when he was called. He was assigned to preach "from this time forth." This revelation for Thomas Marsh was filled with warnings, counsel, and promises not only for his mission but also for his life. Time will show us that it would have been wise for Thomas to have held onto the words of this revelation, much as Josh did with his blessing. The same is true for all of us. When the Lord speaks to us, we would do well to remember His message. —EBF

Reflect and Respond

Take a few minutes to consider a blessing you have been given. What words could you hold onto?

Your favorite scripture in Section 31

DOCTRINE AND COVENANTS 32:3

And I myself will go with them and be in their midst.

This section is directed to a group of men who were called on a mission to the Lamanites, which is what the early members called the American Indian tribes. Someone once asked me to count the number of missionaries being sent on this particular mission. I counted Parley, Oliver, Peter, and Ziba. Four. And then I noticed verse three, in which the Lord said, "I myself will go with them." Five.

Parley P. Pratt had moved to Ohio from New York, his home state, when he was nineteen years old, intending to preach to the American Indian tribes. He wrote in his journal, "I will win the confidence of the [Indian]; I will learn his language; I will tell him of Jesus; I will read to him the Scriptures; I will teach him the arts of peace; to hate war, to love his neighbor, to fear and love God."[8] He had great ambitions, but when he got to Ohio, he never got that chance. He ended up getting married and then deciding to become a traveling preacher back in the New York area. On that trip, he was inspired to get off his canal boat in an unexpected place. When he got off, he met a Baptist deacon who just happened to have a copy of the Book of Mormon, and the rest is history.

As a new member, when Parley overheard about Oliver's and Peter's mission to the Lamanites, he pleaded with Joseph to ask the Lord if he could go too. The Lord was so good and not only called Parley to go with those men (fulfilling at least a five-year-long wish) but then promised that He Himself would go with them. He fulfilled a dream and then added something better. —DB

Reflect and Respond

When have you sensed the Lord's companionship and presence in the different ministries you have been called to?

Your favorite scripture in Section 32

DOCTRINE AND COVENANTS 33:4

. . . save it be a few.

After Ezra Thayre and Northrop Sweet were baptized, they were called to help spread the good news of the gospel in a time when the vineyard had become corrupt and there were not many who were doing good, save it be a few. "Open your mouths," the Lord counseled, "and they shall be filled. . . . Yea, open your mouths . . . and you shall be laden with sheaves . . . , open your mouths and they shall be filled" (D&C 33:8–10). I love this thought of being filled and laden with sheaves because they were serving with the Lord to build His kingdom.

Interestingly, Northrop Sweet soon left the Church to begin his own church. He never opened his mouth to share the gospel he had been given. His congregation consisted of six members and did not grow any more.[9] Ezra Thayre, on the other hand, followed the counsel of the Lord. He opened his mouth and filled his barn with people who came to hear the Prophet speak. The crowd was so big that some could not fit in.

It is an interesting visual of empty and full. Life has taught me that Satan wants to leave us empty, but the Lord wants to fill us. He promises a fulness. This is a blessing not just to be realized in eternity; it is a promise to His servants now.

I consider these two men and realize there is an important lesson here. Not everyone will heed the counsel of the Lord. Not everyone will work with Him to open their mouth and share. Not everyone will introduce others to His gospel, save it be a few.

I want to be counted as one of those few.

And then, I want to fill barns to overflowing. —EBF

Reflect and Respond

How could you open your mouth and share the gospel today? Are you willing to be one of the few?

Your favorite scripture in Section 33

DOCTRINE AND COVENANTS 34:8

And it shall be a great day . . .

I remember jumping into my bed at the end of the day after one of my daughters was baptized. It was a day filled with friends, family, and faith. I lay there and looked up at the ceiling and said to myself, "Today was such a good, good day." Have you had one of those?

Orson Pratt was taught the gospel of Jesus Christ and then later baptized by his brother Parley on September 19, 1830—his nineteenth birthday. That was a good day. Less than a month later, he traveled over 200 miles to Fayette, New York, to meet the Prophet Joseph Smith—another good day. Just like his brother Parley, when he heard about others being called to missions, he wanted Joseph to ask the Lord about a call for him to serve. Joseph agreed, of course, and this section was the revelation that Joseph received from the Lord with Orson sitting there listening as it was dictated.

Orson wrote about that good day: "I thought that was a very great and important calling. . . . I felt, therefore, the importance of those sayings; and truly, when I looked at the magnitude and importance of the *command* given to me to prophesy by the power of the Holy Ghost, I felt oftentimes to tremble and shrink, for fear I never should be able to fulfill and accomplish so great a work."[10] As part of the revelation, the Lord told Orson how blessed he was because he believed. He then told him he was even more blessed because he was being called to preach the gospel (see D&C 34:4–5). And then, to Orson and everyone else reading, the Lord told him that his job was to prepare the people he met for His coming—a day filled with "power and great glory." Because that is going to be "a great day" (D&C 34:7–8). —DB

Reflect and Respond
What happened on your most recent "good day"?

Your favorite scripture in Section 34

DOCTRINE AND COVENANTS 35:3

. . . and prepared thee for **a greater work.**

"Thou art blessed," the Lord told Sidney Rigdon, "*for thou shalt do great things.* Behold thou wast sent forth, even as John, to prepare the way before me, . . . and thou knewest it not." Then He reminded him, "I am God, and mine arm is not shortened; and I will show miracles, signs, and wonders, unto all those who believe on my name" (D&C 35:4, 8; emphasis added). In other words, if you choose to accomplish great things, *I will show up.*

It wasn't true just for Sidney Rigdon. It was true for Moses, and for Peter, and for the brother of Jared, and it's true for me and you. Do you wonder if the Lord has great things in store for you—things that you don't even know about right now? If so, this is a section worth studying, and there are two paradigms you want to look for. Study what happens for those who ask "in faith" in verse nine. Then, contrast them with those "without faith" in verse eleven. What does the Lord teach about the "great things" to be done by the "weak things"(D&C 35:10, 13)?

There are powerful lessons here: a lesson on living in faith compared to living without faith, and, surprisingly, a lesson on recognizing that weakness can be an important part of accomplishing our great things. Is there a great thing you would like to accomplish but you feel like you can't? What is the weakness that makes you think you can't accomplish it? Acknowledging our weakness helps us to know what to ask for from the Lord in order to accomplish the great things He has in store for us. Then we need to act in faith and trust the Lord. He is God.

He will show up. —EBF

Reflect and Respond

Take some time to ponder the great things the Lord has in store for you. Write down any impressions that come.

Your favorite scripture in
Section 35

DOCTRINE AND COVENANTS 36:2

And **I will lay my hand upon you**
by the hand of my servant Sidney Rigdon.

I can remember clearly how powerful the rancher's witness was and the impact it had on my heart. I was in a small meeting in church, and the lesson was being given by a man who wore a mismatched suit coat and pants and scratched-up cowboy boots. He didn't look like much—just a normal grandpa—but when he bore his witness, it came through me like lightning. That experience has happened to me over and over, in a blessing from a dentist, counsel from a hospital administrator, an inspired testimony from a plumber.

When that little group of missionaries was on the way to "Indian Territory" (see section 32), they made a pit stop in Ohio to visit some of Parley P. Pratt's friends and to preach to Sidney Rigdon's Reformed Baptist congregation. Among those intrigued and captivated by the missionary message were a hatmaker named Edward Partridge and his wife, Lydia. She was baptized right away, but Edward decided he wanted to go to New York first to meet Joseph Smith and do some more investigating before he made any commitments.

During a meeting in which Joseph, a farm boy, was preaching, Edward Partridge stood and announced that he had decided to be baptized that very day. He soon received this revelation from the Lord: "I will lay my hand upon you by the hand of my servant . . . and you shall receive my Spirit, the Holy Ghost" (D&C 36:2). The Lord Himself would lay His hand on Edward by the hand of his friend Sidney. I wonder how Edward felt to hear the Lord say that He, personally, would be giving him the gift of the Holy Ghost. I also wonder how he felt knowing that in the future, he, Edward, a hatmaker, would represent the Lord. That his own hands would one day be His hands. —DB

Reflect and Respond

How does it make you feel to know that you have been called to speak and uplift and love in the name of the Lord Himself?

Your favorite scripture in Section 36

DOCTRINE AND COVENANTS 37:1

. . . go to the Ohio.

There is a portrait of Lucy Mack Smith, painted by Henry Inouye, that hangs in the visitors' center adjacent to the Kirtland Temple. She is wearing a soft yellow dress with beautiful ruffles on the bodice. The fine white lace that adorns her bonnet is a stark contrast to her steel-gray hair, and a beautiful choker is pinned to her crisp white collar. However, none of that beauty is what captures your attention when you see the painting. It's her eyes. Piercing, determined, steady. Those eyes look directly into your soul, and she seems to be asking, "Are you up for what lies ahead? Are you equal to the task?" There is no doubt that she was.

When Joseph came home from the grove, she was there. When the Church was organized in the Whitmer home, she was there. When the Kirtland Temple was dedicated, she was there. And when the Lord said, "Go to the Ohio," and no one stepped up to lead the Saints from New York to Kirtland, she was there.

To the chagrin of many, Mother Smith did not back down from her beliefs along that journey, calling for prayer twice a day and singing even when people told her she would be mobbed. In the middle of a torrential downpour, when they told her she would not be able to find a dry place for the mothers and sick children, she not only found a room but shared her beliefs with the woman who owned the establishment. And when the boat became stuck in two feet of ice and could not leave the harbor, she called for the Saints on her boat to pray to the Lord for deliverance, and with a loud clap like thunder, the ice split open enough for her boat to leave the harbor, leaving all the other boats behind.

It didn't matter what she was up against, Lucy was there, equal to the task. —EBF

Reflect and Respond
When has the Lord asked you to do something hard? How did you respond?

Your favorite scripture in
Section 37

DOCTRINE AND COVENANTS 38:31-32

That ye might **escape** the power of the enemy, and be **gathered** unto me a righteous people, . . . **ye should go** to the Ohio; and there I will give unto you my law; and there you shall be endowed with power from on high.

The commandment from the Lord for the Church to move to Ohio came just three days before this more lengthy revelation was received. What would those three days have been like? The first revelation had so few details. In answer to all the questions and the wonderings of why they were moving, the Lord gave them this particular revelation, including these magnificent promises. Why were they going? To escape, to gather, and to receive. I wonder if similar promises are related to all the commandments the Lord gives to us. Have you ever thought of these promises in your own experiences? What is He helping you escape? Where is He gathering you to? What is it that He has ready to pour out upon you?

After the conference where these promises were made, the reactions were as mixed as you would imagine. Some felt that Joseph had invented the revelation, and they refused to receive it as the word of the Lord. Others struggled to come to grips with it and eventually chose to obey. But my favorite response was from Newel Knight, a faithful brother from the Colesville Branch, Joseph's friend. "Having returned home from conference, in obedience to the commandment which had been given, I, together with the Colesville Branch, began to make preparations to go to Ohio. . . . As might be expected, we were obliged to make great sacrifices of our property. . . . Having made the best arrangements we could for the journey, we bade adieu to all we held dear on this earth and in the early part of April started for our destination."[11] The law the Saints would receive in Ohio was the law of consecration, but Newel Knight had already begun to live it. He was prepared to follow the word of the Lord to escape, to gather, and to receive. —DB

Reflect and Respond

Where have you seen the promises of escaping, gathering, and receiving?

Your favorite scripture in
Section 38

DOCTRINE AND COVENANTS 39:10

. . . a blessing so great as you never have known.

It is a modern-day example of the rich young ruler.

In section 39, we meet a man who grew up knowing Christ and even held an important role in the church he currently attended. He was a minister. He knew the commandments. He read the Bible. After hearing Joseph teach, he covenanted with the Lord that he would obey any command the Lord would give to him through Joseph the Prophet. So Joseph asked, and the Lord responded.

"And now, behold, I say unto you, my servant James, I have looked upon thy works and I know thee. . . . Thine heart is now right before me at this time; . . . the days of thy deliverance are come, *if* thou wilt hearken to my voice . . . and be baptized, . . . and you shall receive my Spirit, and a blessing so great as you never have known. And *if* thou do this, I have prepared thee for a greater work" (D&C 39:7–11; emphasis added).

It's those two "ifs" that should catch your eye and grab your attention. Because within days of receiving this revelation, James Covel departed from Fayette without explanation. He walked away from a blessing greater than he had ever known. The Lord told Joseph it was the fear of persecution and the cares of the world that caused him to walk away.

Sometimes we think of the rich young ruler or people like James Covel and we wonder how they could turn and walk away from the greater things. In future days, even Sidney Rigdon would walk away, even though he too had been given the promise of greater things.

The choice is presented to all of us. The Lord invites each of us to labor, build, and bring forth, to experience the great things.

Will you? —EBF

Reflect and Respond
What keeps you from walking away?

Your favorite
scripture in
Section 39

DOCTRINE AND COVENANTS 40:1

Behold, verily I say unto you, that the heart of my
servant James Covel **was right before me.**

James Covel's story isn't retold over and over again. In fact, we don't know much about his story at all. However, there are two revelations about him back-to-back in the Doctrine and Covenants. When you view them side by side, there is a significant one-word difference. On January 5, 1831, the Lord said to Brother James that "thine heart *is* now right before me at this time" (D&C 39:8; emphasis added). One day later, on January 6, the Lord said, "The heart of my servant James Covel *was* right before me" (D&C 40:1; emphasis added).

Don't you wonder what happened in between those two revelations? Why the change? There is such a significant difference between the words *is* and *was*. Those are direction words. Someone once taught me that the direction you are facing in your faith journey today is far more important than where you were yesterday. I believe that is true.

Unfortunately, we don't know what happened on January 7 with Brother James, but if he could change that quickly from the fifth to the sixth, it seems like he could have changed his mind back just as quickly the other way. I love that the Lord refers to him on January 6, when his heart *was* right, as His "servant." I also find a lot of compassion in the ending line of the revelation, when the Lord says, "It remaineth with me to do with him as seemeth me good" (D&C 40:3). James's story isn't over. And neither is ours.

Perhaps someday we will meet James Covel, find out more about his story, and discover that his heart is once again right before the Lord. But today, maybe we could just take a moment once more to examine our own heart and see which word we would choose for ourselves on this day. *Is?* Or *was?* —DB

Reflect and Respond

Would you say that your heart is *or* was *right before the Lord today?*

Your favorite
scripture in
Section 40

DOCTRINE AND COVENANTS 41:12

These words are given unto you . . . ;
beware how you hold them.

In this section we meet a man like unto Nathanael of old. You remember Nathanael, the one whom Jesus saw sitting under the fig tree. The man with no guile. A man with a pure heart. As opposed to those who walked away from the great things, Edward Partridge had a pure heart and remained true. He was called as the first bishop of the Church. When choosing whether to keep his hat shop and his other pursuits or to spend all his time in the labors of the Church, he chose the Church. He was tarred and feathered, spent time in prison, faced poverty, and struggled with physical health, but he held all the words he was given from the Lord close to his heart for his entire life.

In this section, the Lord says, "He that receiveth my law and doeth it, the same is my disciple" (D&C 41:5). Edward was a disciple. "And this because his heart is pure before me" (D&C 41:11).

What does it look like to be known as a disciple of Christ?

What does having a pure heart entail?

How can you be more careful about how you hold the Lord's words?

It's worth considering, because the Lord's promise is sure: "Hearken and hear, O ye my people, saith the Lord and your God, ye whom I delight to bless with the greatest of all blessings, ye that hear me" (D&C 41:1).

Give up the hat shop. Hear the words.

Hold them. —EBF

Reflect and Respond
How can you better hear and hold the words of the Lord?

Your favorite scripture in
Section 41

DOCTRINE AND COVENANTS 42:61

If thou shalt ask, thou shalt receive revelation upon revelation, knowledge upon knowledge, . . . and peaceable things—**that which bringeth joy.**

Have you ever started a new job or moved to a new school or even played a game for the first time? The beginning stages are filled with all sorts of questions.

It was like this for the Saints once they arrived in Ohio. They obeyed the call to move, and the elders obeyed the call to go forth and preach, but once they began, the questions started coming. The Lord had promised them in New York that He would give them His law—teach them how to preach and live as Saints would and should. For each of the questions, the Lord poured out knowledge and revelation that led to peace and joy.

One of the questions the Saints asked about was living according to the New Testament idea of having "all things [in] common" (Acts 4:32). In answer, the Lord of liberal giving taught the Saints how to live with that same spirit. He taught them a system of consecration that would lead to everyone enjoying and living in the bounty the Lord provides. He also taught them how to forgive, how to obey, and how to fulfill responsibility.

The Saints referred to this revelation as "the law," and in the heading we learn that Joseph specified it as "embracing the law." Whenever I first hear the word *law*, it does not give me a warm feel of something I would want to embrace. Laws seem cold, restrictive, and binding. But these laws governed a new way to live—to thrive. A new way to love. And they came from a warm, limitless, good God. Every time I read the phrase "embracing the law" I now change it in my mind to what it actually is: "embracing Him." —DB

Reflect and Respond

In what ways has the Lord guided you through a new stage of life? What revelation, knowledge, peace, and joy has He poured out?

Your favorite scripture in
Section 42

DOCTRINE AND COVENANTS 43:11

Sanctify yourselves.

The counsel to become sanctified is repeated three times in section 43: "Be sanctified by that which you have received, and ye shall bind yourselves to act in all holiness before me" (verse 9); "Purge ye out the iniquity which is among you; sanctify yourselves before me" (verse 11); and "Sanctify yourselves and ye shall be endowed with power" (verse 16).

If you want to know more about this word *sanctify,* there is a reference in Joshua 3:5 that helps: "sanctify yourselves . . ." It is the footnote for the word *sanctify* that brings the clarification, "Make yourselves clean, holy, by ritual washings and proper behavior."

Becoming holy through sanctification happens through ritual washings and proper behavior. Sanctification happens through covenant and law. It isn't coincidental that section 42 contains the law. Within ten months, the Lord would command the Saints to begin the construction of a temple. They received first the law and then the covenant.

I think of this group of Saints, who had traveled so many miles, who had suffered so much persecution, who were experiencing poverty, and I watch the Lord strengthening them through sacrifice. Is that what sanctification looks like? Is that the process of becoming holy?

Bind yourselves to act in all holiness.

Purge out the iniquity.

Then you will be endowed with power.

Power after the purging.

Sanctification. —EBF

Reflect and Respond

How is the Lord sanctifying you?

Your favorite scripture in
Section 43

DOCTRINE AND COVENANTS 44:1-2

It is expedient in me that the elders of my church should be called together, from the east and from the west, . . . by letter **or some other way.** . . . I will pour out my Spirit upon them.

We have both had opportunities to teach in a lot of different settings and places—around campfires, in classrooms, in prisons, and from pulpits. It is often a surprise how many people will actually come, what the setting will look like, and what the teaching conditions will be. It adds some excitement knowing that every assignment will always be a little bit different. But in each of these experiences, the one constant has been the presence of the Lord's Spirit—just as He promised to the elders who were heading on missions years ago.

After a previous revelation sending the missionaries out two by two, a revelation came to gather them back together again—for strength and encouragement. I love that the Lord tells them to come and gather from the east, west, south, or north, by letter, or by some other way. It didn't matter. The thing that mattered was that they would gather in the name of the Lord. And if they did, He promised He would pour out His spirit upon them.

Most recently, the two of us have found "some other way" to gather a community: through YouTube videos and podcasts. Even though we are not physically together, we have felt and experienced the same promise from the Lord—an outpouring of His Spirit. It doesn't matter where or how we assemble, the Lord is interested in meeting us in those places and turning those gatherings into strengthening experiences before He sends us out again to gather more. —DB

Reflect and Respond

When was the last time you gathered with someone in the name of the Lord? Did you experience the promise of His Spirit?

Your favorite scripture in Section 44

DOCTRINE AND COVENANTS 45:57

. . . and have not been deceived.

Do you feel like doing a puzzle? Turn to Matthew 25 and read the parable of the ten virgins. Here is what you should look for: (1) what is entrusted; (2) how long the waiting period is; (3) the separation or division among the groups; (4) how knowing Jesus becomes a determining factor.

In the case of the ten virgins the answers would be: (1) oil; (2) until midnight; (3) foolish and wise; (4) verse 12, which Joseph translated to read, "ye know me not."

Section 45 of the Doctrine and Covenants helps us to understand the ten virgins parable a little bit better by telling us how to be wise, saying, "They that are wise . . . have received the truth, and have taken the Holy Spirit for their guide, and have not been deceived" (D&C 45:57).

This section explains that remaining wise will require us to receive truth *and* the Holy Spirit. Perhaps you could consider some instances during the past week when those two things have been true for you. Section 45 gives one more piece of counsel: we have to work at not being deceived. It is a strong admonition for the world we live in today, because Satan is intent on deceiving us and will use any means to keep us from being wise. He does not want us to gather truth or Spirit because he knows it will help anchor us to Christ. Embracing truth and the Spirit is how we increase the oil we have been entrusted with during this waiting period.

It is how we become known as someone wise. —EBF

Reflect and Respond

How are you doing with the oil you have been entrusted to obtain?
How could truth and the Spirit add to your reserve?

Your favorite scripture in **Section 45**

DOCTRINE AND COVENANTS 46:9

They are **given for the benefit of those who
love me** . . . that all may be benefited.

Every member of the early Church of Jesus Christ was a convert. Each one came from his or her own tradition and style of worship, and the newly restored Church's worship services didn't have much instruction or pattern—just a bunch of enthusiasm. Sometimes it was a little too much for people, and the enthusiasm of some would turn others away. "Some would fancy to themselves that they had the sword of Laban, and would wield it as expert as a light dragoon. . . . Some would slide or scoot and [on] the floor, with the rapidity of a serpent, which the[y] termed sailing in the boat to the Lamanites."[12] Can you imagine?

As crazy as all of this sounds, perhaps the worst practice of all was that some were excluding from the worship services those who were not yet baptized members. In answer to all of this spiritual confusion, the Lord gave this revelation. Most of the revelation explains which spiritual gifts come from the Lord and how to recognize them. But, above all, it was a reminder that the gifts were there to benefit all. Perhaps, in sharing this, the Lord was reminding the Saints that the gifts were also for all of those who would still come. What gifts would those people bring? What benefit would they be to each other? Yes, all of the spiritual gifts are given for a benefit, but spiritual gifts are always brought by people. People are the conduits. Everyone is needed so that everyone can benefit. One of the ways the Lord can show His love to us is by sending spiritually gifted people into our lives. What a shame if we excluded them for any reason! —DB

Reflect and Respond
When have you benefited from the spiritual gift of another?

Your favorite
scripture in
Section 46

DOCTRINE AND COVENANTS 47:3

I have appointed to another office . . .

It was the calling I didn't want: ward organist. I play the piano; I am *not* an organ player. So, for the entire year I had that calling, we would leave for church an hour early so I could practice. Greg would grab my makeup bag on the way out the door so I could reapply my mascara after crying through that one hour of practice. Despite all the practice over that year, I don't think I got one bit better. But I always showed up.

One year later, I got called into the Relief Society, and a year after that was my first time working with the youth. I showed up for each one of those callings—the ones I loved and the ones I didn't love as much.

The thing I love most about section 47 is knowing that people were assigned different places to assist in the work clear back then. John Whitmer was in charge of keeping a history of the Church. Oliver Cowdery was appointed to another office. Everyone serving, wherever they could assist, was what kept the Church moving. They accepted the call and then they showed up.

It makes me wonder where you are serving right now. What is the office you have been appointed to? You might have your favorite calling, or maybe you grab your mascara before you leave the house, just in case. It's all of us assisting together that keeps this work moving forward.

It's all about showing up. —EBF

. . . .

Reflect and Respond
Where are you serving currently? How could you show up?

Your favorite
scripture in
Section 47

DOCTRINE AND COVENANTS 48:2

And inasmuch as ye have lands,
ye shall impart to the eastern brethren.

During a humanitarian trip to Fiji, my nephew Spencer's shirt was torn in a rugby game with local kids. Instinctively one of the boys, Fraser, ran off the field and went all the way home to grab an extra jersey. "Put it on," he insisted as he waved it in Spencer's face. There was a back-and-forth before Spencer finally agreed, slipped it on, and finished the game. It wasn't until a few days later, after seeing Fraser in the same red shirt day after day, that Spencer learned the jersey was the only other shirt the boy owned. But it was extra—and the boy knew Spencer needed a shirt.

This same spirit filled the Saints living in Ohio when they asked the Lord where and how they would find places for the New York Saints to live—the destitute New York Saints who were on their way to Ohio to obey the Lord's command to gather. "Inasmuch as ye have lands, ye shall impart to the eastern brethren," was the answer (D&C 48:2). If you have extra land, give it to your brothers and sisters who are on their way. Simple. And if there is no room, buy up more land to share. When we think of Ohio, we think of the amazing revelations and the Spirit that was poured out on that place. Perhaps it was because there was a people there prepared to receive it. Those miracles landed softly on giving hearts.

Spencer left his whole backpack of shirts when he left Fiji—because they were extra—but he returned home with something more: the jersey he had been given and what it means to impart to a brother. —DB

Reflect and Respond

How have you seen people live this lesson of imparting generously?

Your favorite scripture in Section 48

DOCTRINE AND COVENANTS 49:27

I will go before you and be your rearward;
and I will be in your midst.

Have you ever been to a wilderness place?

Usually it is barren land. Uncharted territory. Stark. Uninhabited and inhospitable. But the Lord loves wilderness places. Their presence is noted throughout all of scripture. Moses and the children of Israel wandered through one for forty years. John the Baptist taught in one. Lehi and Nephi traveled through one.

There is learning that comes from wilderness places, and wilderness places are always a precursor to a promised land.

In the last days, the Lord promises a flourishing in wilderness places. But such blossoming won't happen on its own. The Lord is calling us into those wilderness places to spread the good news.

At the end of the journey of Moses, just before the children of Israel entered into the promised land, the Lord taught an important truth about wilderness places: "He knoweth thy walking through this great wilderness: these forty years the Lord thy God *hath been with thee*; thou hast lacked nothing" (Deuteronomy 2:7; emphasis added). The Lord never leads us into a wilderness place alone. He isn't just watching us walk through that wilderness; He will be there with us to make sure that we lack for nothing.

This same promise is given to the missionaries in section 49: "Behold, I will go before you and be your rearward; and I will be in your midst, and you shall not be confounded" (D&C 49:27).

Are you in a wilderness place? Uncharted territory? An inhospitable situation? Are you waiting to reach the promised land? Look for the Lord. He has promised to be there. —EBF

Reflect and Respond

When have you experienced a wilderness place in your life? Look back at that moment. Do you see signs that the Lord was there?

Your favorite scripture in Section 49

DOCTRINE AND COVENANTS 50:10

Let us reason together,
that ye may understand.

As a parent of young kids, I am often flabbergasted by how unreasonable and irrational children can be. The things that set them off are astounding. Sometimes I hear an emotionally charged sound from the other room and have no idea whether an older sibling looked at them funny or their entire hand has been cut off. The reaction would be the same for either instance. I have one child in particular who can move from an emotional 0 to 10 in about four seconds. My initial reaction with him is always to match his emotion with my frustration. Why is he acting this way? Why can't he be reasonable?

During one particular episode, I watched my wife, Jenny, do something masterful. Instead of talking to this child as if he were full of experience, insisting he act like an adult, she got on his level, took his hands in hers, and spoke calmly and gently through the issue. She approached the problem as if it were completely understandable and reasonable for him to respond that way. So gentle. So tender. It wasn't long before his disposition started to match hers.

The problems we saw in section 46 continued and increased in the Kirtland area once all the leaders left on their missions. The "spiritual manifestations" were outlandish and inappropriate. The members of the Church were young in their faith, and they often showed their spiritual immaturity. Instead of blasting them from heaven, the Lord, in a sense, took their hands in His and reasoned with them until they understood. He slowly walked them through their own experience and education—as He always does. Eventually, their disposition began to match His. They were slowly becoming His people. —DB

Reflect and Respond
When has the Lord tutored you gently and patiently?

Your favorite
scripture in
Section 50

DOCTRINE AND COVENANTS 51:16-17

. . . for a little season . . . as for years . . .

When Jerusalem was destroyed, the people of Jeremiah were carried off into captivity, where they remained for seventy years. When they arrived in the land of captivity, the Lord told them to build houses and plant gardens, to have children and plan weddings, and to pray for the peace of that city. It would have been a hard thing to do: to thrive there, to build and plant and celebrate.

When the Saints arrived in Ohio, the Lord's counsel was the same. He knew they weren't going to stay there forever. They would live in Ohio for just a little season, but He wanted them to act upon this land "as for years" because there was a blessing there for them. He knew building and planting and celebrating in that place would "turn unto them for their good" (D&C 51:17).

The Saints would live in extreme poverty while they were in Ohio. The burdens of financial difficulties and persecution and a church operating in two separate locations would weigh heavily on Joseph and the people. And yet, the Lord would ask them to sacrifice all in order to build a house unto Him. A house that would take five years to build. A house they would leave behind when they left that place.

Their little season was eight years. The blessing that came from their sacrifice was the blessing of a temple in their midst. It was what turned unto them for their good.

I have seen that temple. I have stood inside the great doors and looked up at the spiral staircase. I have read about the manifestation of the Spirit that took place within those walls. Even now, there is beauty there, and peace. It stands today as a symbol of what God can do with our hard seasons of sacrifice. He can bring beauty. He can give peace. —EBF

Reflect and Respond

When has the Lord brought beauty and peace into a season of hardship for you?

Your favorite scripture in Section 51

DOCTRINE AND COVENANTS 52:36

Let them labor with their families, declaring none other
things than the prophets and apostles, that which they have
seen and heard **and most assuredly believe.**

We all gathered together in my mission president's living room. It was less than twenty-four hours after we had arrived in Korea as new missionaries. The room was filled with wide eyes and anticipating hearts. The room was also filled with an equal number of more experienced missionaries. After a semi-tasty and semi-"Americanized" meal, some words of advice, and a prayer, our president teamed us up two by two and sent us out to our new areas.

Section 52 describes a similar situation, with elders being teamed up at a conference held in a large field in Kirtland. Joseph paired up companionships according to a revelation he had received the night before. I wonder if there was an immediate connection and a sense of urgency about their assignments, just as I felt that first morning in Korea.

On that day, most of the companionships were headed west to the borders of the United States—wild territory. Exciting prospects. One companionship, though, was given a unique assignment. Joseph Wakefield and Solomon Humphrey were sent east, back home to "labor with their families." And what would they share? The same message as the rest of the missionaries—the witness of Jesus from the prophets and apostles, what they had seen and heard in their own spiritual journey, and those things they most assuredly believed.

In recent general conferences I have felt a similar sense of urgency to labor in my family, to teach them the words and witnesses of the prophets as found in holy scripture. I have felt to share what I have seen and experienced in my own life, and by consequence the things I most assuredly believe. It is a mission I love, and this time I am particularly happy about who I've been teamed up with. —DB

Reflect and Respond

What are the truths that today you could say you most assuredly believe? How will you share them?

Your favorite
scripture in
Section 52

DOCTRINE AND COVENANTS 53:1

You have called upon me . . .

Sidney Gilbert approached the Lord with one simple question: What did the Lord have in mind for him to do? It is the same question Saul asked on the road to Damascus. Ezra Taft Benson suggests it is the most important question we can ask in our lifetime.[13]

Lord, what would you have me to do?

Following this question, the Lord gave Sidney a list of suggestions:

- Forsake the world
- Receive the Spirit
- Be an agent unto the Church
- Take your journey
- Receive the ordinances
- Labor in the vineyard
- Learn
- Endure to the end

Although they were suggestions that came in answer to a personal question of individual need, the counsel is applicable to all of us. It is counsel that we can learn from and follow. However, that counsel isn't the most important lesson we learn from this section. The most important lesson is that the Lord will answer our individual questions. If we turn to the Lord and ask what He would have us do, He will answer. Perhaps it is time to take a personal inventory. Maybe you could set aside some time to commune with the Lord. Ask what He would have you do, and then be prepared to spend some quiet time listening for His answer. Most often revelation comes in the quiet moments when we are attuned to the Spirit. Answers will come. —EBF

Reflect and Respond

How long has it been since you asked the most important question of this lifetime: "Lord, what wilt thou have me to do?" (Acts 9:6).

Your favorite scripture in Section 53

DOCTRINE AND COVENANTS 54:1

Behold, thus saith the Lord, even Alpha and Omega,
the beginning and the end, even he who was
crucified for the sins of the world . . .

The Saints from the Colesville branch of the Church had not been in the Kirtland area very long before their world was turned upside down once more. The initial call to come to Ohio came so suddenly that the move cost many of them everything. I can almost hear their praises and prayers of thanks when the generous Leman Copley offered his land as a place for them to stay. He had been a member of the Shaker community and then converted to the Church. At great sacrifice, he gave up his land so his destitute fellow Church members would have a place to live. Their prayers had been answered! God was so good! And then, almost as quickly as the kindness had come, Leman decided to return to his Shaker community, and he evicted the Colesville group from his land.

What were they to do? Had God abandoned them? Was their sacrifice worth it?

Perhaps you have been in places like this. Maybe you've experienced times when heaven seemed silent—or worse, when you thought God was intervening, only to find the rug pulled out from under you. These situations can give us a spiritual and emotional whiplash. When Newel Knight, the leader of the Colesville Saints, came to Joseph for help, this revelation is how the Lord responded. His counsel for them was to be patient and included promises of escape that surely brought some comfort. But I have always thought the way the revelation began brought the most comfort of all. He is the beginning and the end. He has everything—including them—in His hands. He knew how the trial would start, and He knows how it will finish. And even He, the greatest of all, also suffered persecution at the hands of His friends. The Lord was reminding them that He knew where they were, and He knew how to get them through. The same is true for me and you. —DB

Reflect and Respond

What do you know from the Lord's life that opens your heart to trust Him a little more with yours?

Your favorite
scripture in
Section 54

DOCTRINE AND COVENANTS 55:5

. . . for this cause you shall take your journey.

William W. Phelps's heart was with the Church as soon as he became acquainted with the Book of Mormon, and from that moment forward he was committed. He was a close friend to the Prophet until there was a small moment when William and Joseph had a falling-out. William was excommunicated, and he became a bitter enemy of the Prophet for a time. After he repented, he wrote to Joseph as the prodigal son. Joseph wrote back, "friends at first are friends again at last."[14] W. W. Phelps remained true to the Church for the rest of his life.

His passioned commitment gave us many of the songs in the hymnbook, including "The Spirit of God." Every time I sing that anthem, I think of the passion and commitment of W. W. Phelps.

William was ordained to do the work of printing, of selecting, and of writing. He was told to take his journey, and the Lord told him it was so he could do this work. Reading that made me want to contemplate my own journey, my cause, and my work.

Do I have passion and commitment to the cause to which I have been called? Am I willing to repent when I get off course? Am I devoted to the work?

I want to feel the Spirit of God like a fire, burning.

I want to sing and shout with the armies of heaven.

I want to be part of this great work until the moment Jesus descends with His chariot of fire.

I want the Lord to extend my understanding.

I want to help spread forth the kingdom of heaven. —EBF

Reflect and Respond

What is your cause, your journey, and your work? How could you be more committed to that work?

Your favorite scripture in
Section 55

DOCTRINE AND COVENANTS 56:4

Wherefore I, the Lord, command and
revoke, **as seemeth me good.**

I once received an impression that I felt certain came from the Lord. Maybe I was wrong, but it made sense and it seemed right. Not long after, I ran into some trouble because of someone's decisions, and everything started to fall apart with the choice I had felt impressed to make. I was surprised because I had felt so good about it. When I prayed about it again, I was surprised that I felt impressed to move in an entirely new direction. I wondered, why didn't God just take me in this direction in the first place? Was the first impression not right?

Something similar is happening in this revelation. The Lord originally commanded Ezra Thayre to go on a mission with Thomas B. Marsh, and for Newel Knight and Selah Griffin to go as companions. Because of a broken promise by Leman Copley (see section 54), Newel Knight now had to lead his people to Missouri, and he couldn't fulfill his assignment. And because Ezra Thayre was wrapped up in the troubles that had happened with the land promises, he was not prepared to go out on his mission either. This new revelation changed the mission assignments.

As frustrating as it may be at times, the Lord allows His children their agency. Sometimes this means that others' choices affect the course of our lives—lives that we felt the Lord was directing. I learned that if something didn't work out, or if I hit a roadblock because of someone's agency, it didn't mean the Lord wasn't leading me, nor did it mean that He had stopped. One thing we can trust—He will keep leading us. He will command and revoke and make adjustments, but He will still lead us. And His motivation? It is good. We can trust that, too. —DB

Reflect and Respond

When has it seemed like the Lord has had to reroute your journey?
What have you learned or been learning from the experience?

Your favorite
scripture in
Section 56

DOCTRINE AND COVENANTS 57:14

. . . and let those of whom I have spoken
be planted *in the land of Zion.*

I love flowers of every kind, but I have a favorite: peonies. I love them. I can't get enough of them. Sadly, they are available for only a couple of weeks every year, which makes them even more special. My life revolves around those two weeks.

One year, I accidentally planned a trip to Mexico for the two weeks the peonies were going to be in bloom. My heart nearly failed when I realized it. I couldn't miss the event that happens only one time a year, so I cut three dozen of those peony buds and put them in a vase. I made my good friend hold that vase on her lap for the entire drive down to Mexico. (That is a *good* friend.) When we arrived, I put that vase right next to my bed so that I wouldn't miss one minute of that year's peony harvest.

I love peonies so much that every year I add a few new plants to the yard. It takes two years for those new plants to bloom, but I am patient, and I wait, because I know what it is ahead, and I know it's going to be good.

I wonder if that was what it was like when the Lord started building up Zion in the center place. He planted Sidney Gilbert there to establish a store. He planted William W. Phelps there to be a printer. And there were others who would be planted, as speedily as could be, with their families to help build Zion (see D&C 57:14).

The scriptures hint that the same planting will take place at a future day. The Lord will assign people to be planted in New Jerusalem because He knows what it is ahead, and He knows it's going to be good. It is the land that He has "appointed and consecrated for the gathering of the saints" (D&C 57:1). But it isn't time yet. Until that time, He has asked us to bloom right where we are. We need to do the work He has set out for us there. —EBF

Reflect and Respond

Where have you been planted? What is the work God needs you to be doing there?

Your favorite scripture in Section 57

DOCTRINE AND COVENANTS 58:6

*For this cause I have sent you—that you might be obedient, and that your hearts might **be prepared to bear testimony** of the things which are to come.*

The letter that Lydia Partridge opened from her husband did not include the happy news she was probably hoping for. Edward Partridge had gone with Joseph Smith and several of the other elders to Missouri and had planned on staying a little while before returning home. Instead, the Lord gave Edward and his family a new calling—to move to and manage the lands purchased near Independence. To "lay the foundation" of the future city of Zion. In his letter requesting Lydia to move with their five daughters out to where Edward was, he told her, "We have to suffer & shall for some time many privations here which you & I have not been much used to for year[s]."[15] Despite the promised trouble, Lydia came. It was in her nature to do so. Perhaps the words from this revelation gave her the strength to do so. Those words were a call to be obedient as well as an instruction to prepare her heart for a testimony that she would bear later. Edward had promised difficulties, but the Lord had set her heart on anticipating a testimony that would come.

The Partridge family most certainly suffered many things as a result of the calling the Lord gave them. Their accommodations on the frontier were not what they were used to, and they were met with severe persecution from outside the Church and intense trouble from within it while serving to build up the city of Zion. It makes me want to hear what Lydia would say today. As she prepared her heart to obey the Lord through such hardship, what did she experience and feel? How did it prepare her to bear testimony?

Where has the Lord sent you?

How is your heart being prepared to bear testimony? —DB

Reflect and Respond

What have you been through that you can now look back on and bear testimony about?

Your favorite scripture in
Section 58

DOCTRINE AND COVENANTS 59:5

Thou shalt **love the Lord thy God** with all thy heart.

We can't underestimate the commandments of God. The giving of those commandments is in our earliest scripture. You remember Moses going to the top of Mount Sinai, carving the words into the stone—it was the introduction of God's law. Deuteronomy contains the second giving of the law. The first five books of scripture contain a record of the people as they learned how to live that law.

When Nephi returned to Jerusalem to obtain the plates, he would have gone back for those same five books of scripture. Besides those first books, the Book of Mormon also contains words of prophets giving their perspective of those first laws and commandments.

For the Saints living in the latter days, the Doctrine and Covenants does the same thing. In section 59 we read about this law—the same law given by the same God of Moses. As we read through the Doctrine and Covenants, we watch a modern-day people who are given a new perspective of living God's Old Testament law.

Lessons like this remind us how constant God is—unchanging even after thousands of years.

It might be fun to look at both accounts of the giving of the law. Take some time to compare Exodus 20 and Doctrine and Covenants 59. Read all of both chapters. Make note of what you learn. What are the similarities? What are the differences? What do you learn about God and His commandments as you look at both accounts side by side? —EBF

Reflect and Respond

What would you write in your own personal record of living by the law? What blessings and challenges have you experienced?

Your favorite scripture in Section 59

DOCTRINE AND COVENANTS 60:13

Behold, they have been sent to preach my gospel....
Thou shalt not idle away thy time, neither shalt
thou bury thy talent that it may not be known.

Part of the group that gathered in Missouri for the dedication of the land of Zion were the elders the Lord had sent on missions to the western edge of the United States. They all left around the same time, but some got there much quicker than the rest of them because they had not really stopped along the way to preach the gospel to those they were passing. In this section, the Lord reminded them that "I am able to make you holy, and your sins are forgiven you" (D&C 60:7). That is such good news! And that is the message they were being sent with: the good news that God can make the common people of this world holy and can forgive them of their sins. It was a message that everyone needed to hear.

In New Testament times, the Lord gave a parable, recorded in Matthew 25, about a master who gave His servants talents. In the parable, one of the servants buries his talent in the ground. Because of the word translation, some modern readers might think the Lord was talking about burying some sort of skill or ability. But remember, a talent is money—it represents the business of the master. And what is the great Master's business? People. He is in the business of making people holy. The Lord was making a reference to this parable when He reminded these missionaries not to bury the mission God gave them by passing on people—His greatest treasure. Instead, they were to invite people to holiness by preaching the gospel to them. As they started their journey back home, He was giving them this reminder and advice: Don't be so quick to get to your mission that you miss your actual mission. —DB

Reflect and Respond

Are you so busy getting things done that you have missed the chance to be about the Lord's business—the lifting and loving of people?

Your favorite
scripture in
Section 60

DOCTRINE AND COVENANTS 61:22

It mattereth not unto me . . .

This is a great section for obtaining a better understanding of prayer and revelation and God. In this section, we watch God work in two separate ways, and both examples strengthen our understanding of how God communicates with His children.

First, the Lord told some of the men who were traveling to Zion, "It mattereth not unto me . . . whether they go by water or by land; let this be as it is made known unto them according to their judgments" (D&C 61:22). On the other hand, a little later the Lord says, "Behold, I, the Lord, have appointed a way for the journeying of my saints; and behold, *this is the way*—that after they leave the canal they shall journey by land" (D&C 61:24; emphasis added). It is important to note that sometimes the Lord tells us the way He wants us to do things, and sometimes He says, *it mattereth not,* and we are left to our best judgment in that situation.

Maybe you are wondering how to know which situation you are in: whether you should wait for the Lord to tell you what to do or move forward with your best judgment. Verse 28 provides the answer: "Wherefore, let him do as the Spirit of the living God commandeth him, whether upon the land or upon the waters. . . . Be of good cheer, . . . for I am in your midst, and I have not forsaken you" (D&C 61:28, 36).

The Lord has promised that He will journey with us and that the Spirit of the living God will be with us so we will know what to do. I love knowing we do not travel alone. In the crucial moments, God will tell us the way, and at other times He will stand beside us, trust our judgment, and cheer us on. —EBF

Reflect and Respond
When have you used your best judgment to make a decision between several workable options? When has the Lord told you the way?

Your favorite scripture in Section 61

DOCTRINE AND COVENANTS 62:3

Nevertheless, ye are blessed, for **the testimony which ye have borne is recorded in heaven** for the angels to look upon; and they rejoice over you, and your sins are forgiven you.

I have never accidentally crossed paths with the prophet, but a friend of mine has. They happened to be at the same meeting, and not only did they get to take a picture together, but the meeting ended with a blessing upon those who were there. It thrilled my friend to be there and to hear what the prophet said to him. It was on a day he needed it.

Something similar happened to the group of elders this revelation was directed toward. They were on their way to their mission out west. Joseph and his group were traveling back east from Missouri to Ohio, and they all met each other by chance on the banks of the Missouri River. That is where Joseph gave them this blessing and direction from the Lord. I imagine that, like most new missionaries, parents, or teachers, they were feeling a little inadequate with their assignment. It is so easy to feel underqualified in the work of the Lord. These words that the Lord spoke to them thrill my heart today—especially as I try my best to teach my own children the glorious gospel. Am I doing it well enough? To these new, inexperienced elders, the Lord said their testimony was "recorded in heaven for angels to look upon; and they rejoice over you" (D&C 62:3). Could their testimonies be that good already—so good that an angel would want to read and reread and rejoice over them? The good news of this revelation from the Lord is the answer: "Yes!"

The first word of this verse is *nevertheless*. It is so encouraging. Their missions were not completed yet, but He was already so very thrilled with what they were doing.

Perhaps you and I should believe the same about our own individual missions—whatever they may be. They may not be finished, but they are already accepted and adored. —DB

Reflect and Respond

What witness from an inexperienced source has led you to rejoice? What encouragement does that give you about your own witness?

Your favorite scripture in
Section 62

DOCTRINE AND COVENANTS 63:61

Let all men beware **how they take my name . . .**

I am intrigued by what it *means* to take the Lord's name in vain. Sometimes we use this phrase as a lesson on swearing, but I think there is a greater lesson here—a lesson on authority, intention, and care.

The Greek word for "name" is *onoma,* which can also mean "authority." So, when we read the phrase *take my name upon you,* we could change it to read *take my authority upon you.* Consider some situations when you might do that. Every Sunday, when we take the sacrament, we covenant that we are willing to take the name of the Son, to always remember Him and keep His commandments. Our taking of the bread is symbolic of our accepting this covenant, but do we accept it in vain? Is our promise hollow or lacking substance or worth? Are we planning on doing something with that name? With that authority?

How committed are we to taking the name of Jesus Christ?

There are so many blessings that come through His name—power, the ability to minister, the authority to prophesy in His name. It is a refuge. We gather in His name and call on His name. By His name devils are cast out, miracles happen, deliverance comes. We believe, become, and have life through His name. The Holy Ghost comes in His name. We are made whole, saved, and receive a remission of sins in His name. We take His name by baptism, through covenant, and we worship in His name.

"Remember that that which cometh from above is sacred, and must be spoken with care" (D&C 63:64).

We must be mindful about how we take His name. —EBF

Reflect and Respond

As you take the sacrament this week, prepare yourself to take His name and then to act as His witness throughout the week.

Your favorite scripture in Section 63

DOCTRINE AND COVENANTS 64:33-34

Be not weary in well-doing, for ye are laying the foundation of a great work. And out of small things proceedeth that which is great. Behold, the Lord requireth the heart and a willing mind.

When I was serving as a bishop, one of my dearest friends was serving as the Primary president in our ward. I remember someone warning us that we would one day not like each other after serving together in those callings. I didn't believe it. Neither did she. For the record, it never happened. Although I think the warning was a little funny, I also think I know what the person was perhaps warning us about. People are just people—and that can be disappointing.

Ezra Booth, an early missionary, became disenchanted with Joseph and the work of the Lord. He saw Joseph and Edward Partridge get into an argument with each other, and it left him unsettled.[16] He also was underwhelmed by the lack of success he found preaching the gospel. Ezra Booth eventually turned against the Prophet, and his disenchantment seems to have stemmed from these initial experiences—experiences that did not meet his demands or expectations.

This revelation, given during a time of questions about future missionary work, the fate of Kirtland and Missouri, and the issues of disappointment, reminded the Saints how important it was to forgive and have compassion (see D&C 64:2, 7). It reminded them that Joseph was not perfect, but God was not requiring perfection. All He was asking of them was to give their heart and willing mind. He encouraged them to keep going because, out of their small efforts, God was going to build something magnificent.

This is such wonderful advice to those who expect too much of themselves or others. Don't be weary of doing good. Perhaps we could add a charge not to be weary of thinking good about others who are doing their small, best jobs at the work of the Lord. —DB

Reflect and Respond

What does it look like in your circumstances to give your heart and willing mind in a small but consistent way?

Your favorite scripture in Section 64

DOCTRINE AND COVENANTS 65:4

Pray unto the Lord, **call upon his holy name . . .**

Whenever something is wrong in our home, I text my friend Nish and tell her to light the candle.

She has a tradition I love. When someone is in desperate need of prayers, she lights a candle in her kitchen. Then, every time she walks past the candle and sees the light flickering, she stops and prays. She has lit the candle in our behalf for Broncos games, for health emergencies, and for times of great sorrow. There is no need too great or too small for the lighting of the candle. If we are praying, Nish wants to pray with us.

I believe in the power of unified prayer. I have seen the miracles that have come because someone thought to pray. That is why I love the end of this verse so much, "Pray unto the Lord, call upon his holy name, make known his wonderful works among the people" (D&C 65:4). Don't you love how He sets up the expectation for us? We can expect that wonderful works will follow prayer and calling upon His holy name, but there is more. He wants us to testify when we experience the wonderful works that follow those prayers.

Who needs your prayers today?

Light a candle in the kitchen.

Call upon His holy name. —EBF

Reflect and Respond

When have you experienced His wondrous works after calling upon His name? How could you make that known?

Your favorite scripture in
Section 65

DOCTRINE AND COVENANTS 66:4

And now, verily, I, the Lord, will show unto you what I will
concerning you, or **what is my will concerning you.**

My whole life, I grew up knowing there was a prophet on the earth. I have often wondered what it is like for someone to hear about that for the first time.

William McLellin was a schoolteacher who came across the restored gospel and heard of the role of Joseph Smith as a prophet in the summer of 1831. He wanted to test whether Joseph was actually a prophet. In his own journal, he wrote that he "went before the Lord in secret, and on my knees asked him to reveal the answer to five questions through his Prophet."[17] Then, without telling the Prophet about his prayer, William asked for a revelation—it was a revelation that answered every one of his five questions.

William would eventually leave the Church. He would even join the mobs that forced the Saints out of their homes. He would ask to fight Joseph with a club. Surely, the Lord knew all of those things were ahead. And still, He had time for those five questions.

What I love most about this story is that we discover the Lord cares about our five questions, whatever they might be, and He intends to answer them. A seminary-teacher friend of mine had a girl approach him one day after class telling him she was thinking of leaving her faith. In an inspired invitation, my friend asked her if she would be willing to try an experiment. General conference was coming up, and he asked her if she would write down all of her questions beforehand, go into the weekend with prayer, fasting, and humility, and then come back and report on Monday. When she returned, like William, she had a notebook filled with answers to every one of her questions.

This is not always how the Lord does it, but the promise is still valid: He will find a way to show us His will—particularly His will concerning us. —DB

Reflect and Respond
What are your five questions?

Your favorite
scripture in
Section 66

DOCTRINE AND COVENANTS 67:3

... but, behold, verily I say unto you
there were fears in your hearts ...

Sometimes I hold things back from the Lord. I feel myself doing it. I tell Him, "Here, see what you can do with these things, these problems and situations—I'm turning them over to you. But, don't touch *this*. I don't want you to get involved with *this*. Because I'm not sure what you are going to do with *this*." It's funny that I think I will do a better job. Really, I just want control over the things I don't know what He will do with.

The Lord begins this section by reminding the Saints who He is. *I've heard your prayers. I know your hearts. I recognize all of the desires you have placed before Me.* "Behold and lo, mine eyes are upon you, and the heavens and the earth are in mine hands, and the riches of eternity are mine to give" (D&C 67:2). *I know who you are,* He reminds them, *do you remember who I am? I see you. I hold heaven and earth in my hands. I can give anything. And yet, there was fear in your hearts.*

There are so many times He could say that to me.

Put aside your fears, He tells them, *and you will come to know me* (see D&C 67:10).

I know it is true. But why is it so hard? Why is my first response fear over faith?

I love when the Lord tells the Saints, "Let not your minds turn back" (D&C 67:14). Because it is all in our minds, fear and faith. It's whatever we talk ourselves into. I worry with the best of them. I know how to feed my fear. I am expert at that. But I also know what it takes to build my faith. I know the process that leads me to look to Him. I have experienced great triumphs in my life by putting my faith in Him.

This section reminds me that if I want to live with faith in my heart, intentionally, then I must remember who He is. —EBF

Reflect and Respond

Where is a place in which you could put faith over fear right now? How can you intentionally do that?

Your favorite scripture in
Section 67

DOCTRINE AND COVENANTS 68:4

And whatsoever they shall **speak when moved upon by the Holy Ghost** shall be scripture, shall be the will of the Lord, shall be the mind of the Lord, shall be the word of the Lord.

I really love imagining what happened behind the scenes with revelations like this. From what we know of the history,[18] during a conference in Ohio, at some point, Orson Hyde, Luke S. Johnson, Lyman E. Johnson, and William E. McLellin took the Prophet aside to ask about the Lord's will for them. I love their desire. I have found myself in the same place—wondering what God would want me to do in a particular situation or season. The Lord answered these men's question and then addressed two other groups of people as well: bishops and parents. It is intriguing to me that the advice He would give to the traveling elders is the same advice He would give to other leaders and to parents. The advice: seek the Holy Ghost. This gift enables missionaries, leaders, and parents to teach and act on the will of the Lord to those they love. I have had one-on-one conversations with my kids in which I desperately wanted power to penetrate their hearts. So many Young Women leaders want to speak the word of the Lord to encourage the young women they serve. And bishops sit behind a desk and seek to be thinking the thoughts that God has for the person they are counseling.

My friend told me today that before she enters into conversations with people, she always prays for the Holy Ghost to lead her and guide her in the conversation. This is the advice the Lord gave to four elders, future leaders, and parents everywhere. It is advice that brings the gentle power and the loving will of God into any kind of situation. —DB

Reflect and Respond

Have you felt moved upon by the Holy Ghost recently? What happened beforehand that contributed to you being open to this?

Your favorite scripture in Section 68

DOCTRINE AND COVENANTS 69:8

...for the good of the church,
and for the rising generations.

I recently received a text that said, "I'm not sure if I believe in the Church anymore." It was from a boy just a few years past his mission, and I wanted to text back, "You do." But I didn't. I started asking questions. I met him where he was.

We've had several conversations since that first text. There will be many more to come. People don't choose to leave the Church in one day, and they don't often choose to come back in one day either. Choosing to believe is an ongoing journey, and it's better when you aren't walking it alone.

This experience has made me realize that belief is never an independent adventure. Believing comes with community. We build and strengthen each other. We lift and we bear burdens and we comfort and we minister. Belief is relational. We love because God loves us. Belief is about people. His people. And it's about bringing others to Him.

In this section, the Lord tells John Whitmer to "travel many times from place to place, and from church to church, . . . preaching and expounding, writing, copying, selecting, and obtaining" (D&C 69:7–8). I hear Him inviting John to be with the people in all their places, to be with the communities of the Church and teach them and encourage them. "For the good of the church, and for the rising generations" (D&C 69:8).

It's not about you. It's about building the kingdom. It's about lifting the next generation.

Go out and do some good. —EBF

Reflect and Respond

What could you do for the good of the Church? How could you lift someone of the rising generation?

Your favorite scripture in Section 69

DOCTRINE AND COVENANTS 70:12

…the same is worthy of his hire, even as **those who
are appointed to a stewardship.**

I remember driving away from the hospital with my brand-new son triple-buckled
into the back seat wondering how and why the nurses and doctors thought it was a good
idea to put this little life into our care. (The truth was, they trusted Jenny.) I think it was
the first time I began to understand the word *stewardship.* I knew he was not technically
ours. God had sent him to our home with His trust to love him as if he were ours. To
watch over and take care of him as He would. To try to help him increase in all capacities
of life and then to teach him to do the same for others. To take all the extra and pass it
along.

Joseph and others learned something about stewardship when they went to the Lord
for instructions after deciding to print a book of the revelations the Prophet had received
so far for the Church. The Lord gave a small group stewardship over the revelations (see
D&C 70:3). They were His words, but He wanted those men to care for and look over
them. He wanted them to protect them, print them, and get them into the hands of the
people—to distribute the truths and help them to increase in the world.

At first, stewardship seems overwhelming. I almost want to quit when I think of the
Lord handing these things over to me. It is too much responsibility. But with it comes a
promise, both of mercy and of abundance—"which abundance is multiplied unto them
through the manifestations of the Spirit" (D&C 70:13). Joseph and the group saw the
abundance as they did the work of the scriptures, and I have seen it when watching over
my own stewardships. Sometimes blessings don't multiply in the ways we had envisioned,
but we do experience an increase every time we engage in His holy work. —DB

Reflect and Respond

*What abundance of spiritual manifestations have you experienced
as you have invested time, money, and care into your stewardships?*

Your favorite
scripture in
Section 70

DOCTRINE AND COVENANTS 71:3

This is a mission **for a season.**

It had been a particularly hard year. We knew it was going to be; we had been prepared in a priesthood blessing my husband had received. It wasn't a surprise to any of us, but that didn't make it less hard. There were sleepless nights, and tears, and so many prayers.

One afternoon, when I was making lunch at the kitchen counter, my son sat down on a stool and said, "Mom, why has the Lord blessed me with such a hard season?" His wife started laughing and said, "Why did you use the word *blessed*?" We all laughed for a minute, and then the conversation turned serious as we started recognizing the blessings that had come from that hard season. It wasn't hard to see the blessings. There was one in particular: a man who had reached out in a time of need to help. That man had become a dear friend to our son. Honestly, I don't know what we would have done without him. And we wouldn't have found him if we hadn't been *blessed* with that hard season.

In section 71, the Lord talks to Joseph about the hard season he is in. In an effort to repair the damage Ezra Booth is doing through saying bad things about the Church, the Lord is sending Joseph on a "mission for a season." The Lord tells him to prepare for the revelations and power that are to come. He counsels Joseph to meet up with his enemies. "Let them bring forth their strong reasons against the Lord," He tells Joseph, " . . . there is no weapon that is formed against you shall prosper" (D&C 71:8–9).

The same is true for each of us. The Lord will bless us in our hard seasons. We will be given revelations and power. As we stand up to our enemies with the Lord, no weapon formed against us will prosper. In the Lord's own due time, the season will end, and there will be good things to come. —EBF

Reflect and Respond

Look back over the hard seasons of your life. What blessings do you recognize from those times?

Your favorite scripture in Section 71

DOCTRINE AND COVENANTS 72:12

That this also may be consecrated to the good of
the church, **to the poor and needy.**

"I cannot see a Bishop in myself, but if you say it's the Lord's will, I'll try." Those were the words of Newel K. Whitney to Joseph Smith after he was called to be the second bishop of the Church. Edward Partridge, the first bishop, was living in and handling the affairs of the Church in Missouri. There was now a need for another bishop in Ohio, and Newel K. Whitney was the man. The task was daunting. The revelations were being printed at great expense, there was persecution from people who had left the Church, there were properties in Ohio and Missouri to manage, and there were families working full-time for the Church who needed sustaining. Newel said to his wife, Ann, that "it would require a vast amount of patience, of perseverance and of wisdom to magnify his calling." How true that would be. Perhaps he relied on the message he heard from the Lord after praying when he received his call: "Thy strength is in me."[19]

Perhaps you have wondered how and why the Lord has given you a particular assignment. Sometimes you feel overwhelmed by the challenges you see. The rest of this revelation gave specific instructions to Bishop Whitney on matters that were particular to that time and place. He sought for them and heeded them because he didn't know how to go forward. The Lord has given and will give instruction and direction for the good of the Church—both to leaders and to members who need it. All of us may feel at times like Newel K. Whitney—poor and in need—but it is in those conditions that we can more clearly hear the Lord's directions, leading us to the good we desire. —DB

Reflect and Respond

Have you ever felt poor in experience or in great need of help? How did that lead to good?

Your favorite scripture in Section 72

DOCTRINE AND COVENANTS 73:4

. . . inasmuch as it is practicable . . .

I was walking down the street one day when a lady grabbed me by the arm. "You don't know me," she said, "but I have to ask you something. How do you get all the studying in? I watch you, and I think you must have figured it out. How do you get it all done?"

"I don't do it all on the same day," was the first thing I told her. Because I don't. On Sundays, I study *Come, Follow Me*. On Thursdays, I study the topics that felt important to my personal circumstances from general conference. On the other days, I try to read ten to twenty minutes from whatever book of scripture I feel drawn to on that day.

"Really?" she said. "You don't do everything every single day?" I shook my head. Just the thought of that overwhelms me. I don't believe in a scorekeeping God. I believe in a God who says to do what you can, when you can, "inasmuch as it is practicable" (D&C 73:4). Does He want me in the scriptures? Of course He does. He knows that reading the scriptures is one of the very best ways to improve my communication with the Holy Ghost. So I read *something* every day because I need that added influence every day.

Section 73 helps us to better understand this principle. "It is expedient to translate again," the Lord tells Joseph Smith and Sidney Rigdon, who are working on the Bible translation, "and, inasmuch as it is practicable, to preach in the regions round about. . . . Let this be a pattern" (D&C 73:3–5). It's such a great pattern. I love that the Lord trusts us to figure out how to do what works with our circumstances. I also love how at the end He tells Joseph, "Gird up your loins" (D&C 73:6). There's no excuse for becoming idle. There is work to be done. But the Lord wants it to be work that exhilarates us, not exhausts us. Be practical. Find balance. Gird up your loins. —EBF

Reflect and Respond

Have you taken the time to figure out a practical schedule for building your spirituality? What does it look like?

Your favorite scripture in Section 73

DOCTRINE AND COVENANTS 74:7

But little children are holy, being sanctified through the atonement
of Jesus Christ; **and this is what the scriptures mean.**

One of the ongoing projects that Joseph Smith was involved in was an inspired translation of the Bible. We know it today as the Joseph Smith Translation. He did not translate the Bible from one language to another, but rather gave commentary, answered questions, and presented new, clearer meanings for verses found in the King James Bible. One of the purposes of the translation work seems to have been to discover the intention of the Bible's original writers.

Historians are not confident about what Joseph's question was, but we do know that the Prophet sought to know the meaning of a difficult phrase found in Paul's letter to the Corinthians. At first, it seems like the New Testament scripture is about marriage between believers and unbelievers (see 1 Corinthians 7:14). Perhaps Joseph was questioning what that meant and what was appropriate in our day. However, the last verse in the revelation gives a new purpose and meaning to the original verse. It gets to the heart of the issue. The Lord taught Joseph that whatever the original circumstances were surrounding Paul's writings, the point was that "little children are holy" because of His atoning sacrifice. When I read the line, "This is what the scriptures mean," I can almost hear Him say, *This is the heart of the issue.* This is why scriptures are written and translated: to lead to that truth. When Joseph asked about clarification, the answer came as another witness about how good the Lord is, how wide His saving arms stretch. That is what the scriptures mean. That is what they were written to teach. —DB

Reflect and Respond

When has pondering over scripture lead you to discover a profound truth?

Your favorite
scripture in
Section 74

DOCTRINE AND COVENANTS 75:19

Leave your blessing upon that house.

Several years ago, we had the opportunity to visit a small church situated in the middle of an old dump in Tijuana, Mexico. After serving a free breakfast to the community, we went to visit some of the homes and leave food and supplies with several of the families from the church of God located there. When we got to one particular home, we stopped to talk with the mother. She told us how hard it was to raise a family in that place, how they never felt safe, how she could hear drug deals going on outside her one-room shack all night long.

She talked about trying to raise good kids, to provide a place of safety. She cried as she told us how hard it was to be a single mother there. We asked her if we could say a prayer before we left, and she agreed. I turned to my neighbor, who was on the trip with us, and asked if he thought it might be appropriate to ask if we could actually dedicate her home. He spoke to her in Spanish and explained what a priesthood blessing of dedication over a home would mean. Again, tears coursed down her face, and she nodded her head yes.

I will never forget that moment as we all stood in a circle and my neighbor evoked the power of the priesthood, asking God to be with that mother and her little children and dedicating that tiny space as a place of refuge and safety.

As we walked down the garbage-lined path back to our cars, my neighbor and I talked. We are probably the only members from The Church of Jesus Christ of Latter-day Saints that woman will ever meet in her lifetime. We had ten minutes to offer her God's best, and we did. We left a blessing upon that house. A priesthood blessing. God's blessing.

Safety and refuge. It is a moment I will never forget. —EBF

Reflect and Respond

Have you ever had an opportunity to leave a blessing on someone's house? What do you remember about that experience?

Your favorite scripture in Section 75

DOCTRINE AND COVENANTS 76:42

That **through him all might be saved** whom
the Father had put into his power . . .

On the first Christmas morning, angels burst through the night sky to proclaim "good tidings of great joy, which shall be to all people" (Luke 2:10). What news could be so good that it would prompt a heavenly choir to fill the clouds above? What truth could cause shepherds to run from house to house declaring it? What news could bring wise men from far away to worship? It is the same truth that caused a stir in the early Church when the Lord's angel-prophet revealed similar good news to the world in this revelation: news of a Savior of all mankind.

While working on the inspired translation of the Bible, Joseph came across a verse about resurrection. It was in the pondering and asking about those scriptures that this particular vision came bursting upon Joseph and his scribe, Sidney Rigdon. The glorious vision they saw and the spectacular truth they learned that all of God's children, except for a few categorized as sons of perdition, would be saved in a kingdom of glory inspired several different reactions from Saints and neighbors.[20] Some could not accept a belief that differed from their traditional view of heaven and hell. Others seemed to share the hearts of the Christmas angels and rejoice in a Savior who was willing and able to save all whom the Father would give Him. All! Of all the truths the Lord revealed to the earth through Joseph, the Prophet once recorded that "nothing could be more pleasing to the Saint, upon the order of the kingdom of the Lord, than the light which burst upon the world, through the . . . vision."[21] February 16, 1832, can be marked as a good day in this history of the world. It was a day that brought some of the best news to all of mankind. —DB

Reflect and Respond

What truths of the gospel have caused your heart to rejoice? Why do you think this revelation was so difficult for some to accept?

Your favorite
scripture in
Section 76

DOCTRINE AND COVENANTS 77:6

What are we to understand . . . ?

When I was growing up, people would commonly suggest that it wasn't worth reading the book of Isaiah or the book of Revelation. Both books were too hard to understand. They worried that trying to get through them would make people my age never want to read the scriptures again. It had the opposite effect on me; it made me want to read those books more.

I don't like it when people tell me I can't do something. There is something in my soul that takes that challenge and runs with it. I was fifteen years old the first time I read Isaiah all the way through. My first attempt at the book of Revelation was one year later. I love both books. They are some of my favorite parts of scripture, and I study them both regularly. There are similar things I love about both: they are detailed and beautiful accounts, I love to look for the descriptions of Jesus Christ, I love unlocking the figurative writing and focusing on the symbolism, and I love that every time I enter in, the Spirit doesn't disappoint but gives me something new to consider within the reading.

Section 77 is a witness that the book of Revelation can be unlocked to our understanding. This revelation was given sometime after April 1832, and on the very oldest copy its title reads, "Revelation Explained."[22] The part that intrigues me the most is that Joseph doesn't get a full explanation of the book of Revelation in the section, he receives answers only to the questions he asks. The same will be true for us. The Lord will help us understand His word; He will speak to us in our own language. Through the Spirit, the Lord will make known to us the answer to our questions.

He doesn't just listen to our questions. He responds. —EBF

Reflect and Respond

When was the last time the Spirit helped you to better understand a passage of scripture? What did you learn from the process?

Your favorite scripture in Section 77

DOCTRINE AND COVENANTS 78:17

Ye have not as yet understood **how great blessings the Father hath** in his own hands and prepared for you.

Joseph Smith was twenty-six years old when he received this particular revelation. Part of the membership of the Church lived in Ohio, and part was building up Zion in Missouri. The revelations received so far were in process of being printed in Missouri, missionary work was causing more and more people to come to Kirtland, financial troubles plagued the growing Church, and Joseph was trying to care for the affairs of the kingdom *and* the poor and needy under his watchful care. How could all of these concerns, and more, not weigh heavily on his mind?

Although I couldn't compare my situation to Joseph's, perhaps I can relate to some degree. I can remember sitting at my kitchen table late one night as a father in my late twenties. The burden of caring for my wife and kids, my new Church calling, my career, my struggling finances, personal weaknesses, and worries about the future pressed upon my mind. The balance felt so fragile. I thought that at any moment all of this could come crashing down.

Perhaps Joseph had similar thoughts. He taught me a pattern throughout his life that I hope to follow more closely—to turn to the Lord for specific help and direction. This revelation was an answer to some of the concerns he and the Church were facing at that time. The word *prepare* shows up at least eight times in the revelation. The first instance was an instruction to Joseph and the Saints—to "prepare yourselves by doing the things which I have commanded" (D&C 78:7). The rest of the times, though, were in reference to what the Lord was preparing *for* the Saints. How comforting it must have been for Joseph to hear that the Father had him in His hands and was preparing the path in front of him. —DB

Reflect and Respond

When have you seen the way prepared before you? What have you learned about the Lord's preparations in comparison to yours?

Your favorite scripture in Section 78

DOCTRINE AND COVENANTS 79:3

I will crown him again with sheaves.

Jared Carter was not a farmer when this revelation was given, he was a missionary. When the Lord talked about sheaves, He wasn't talking about bundles of grain stalks tied together after the harvest, He was talking about bundles of people.

It was a harvest that would make Jared Carter's heart glad.

I can't help but ask myself, *Has the Lord ever crowned you with bundles of people?*

I've been thinking a lot about this. I am reminded of the group of twelve-year-old girls I served when I was in a class presidency as a Beehive. How is it that I can still remember those meetings from when I was twelve years old? The girls' faces? Our adviser? I think of the group of freshman girls at BYU to whom I taught Relief Society lessons. The young mothers I served in our young married ward. The girls I watched over as I served in the Young Women program over the years. The five moms who lost their babies. The Sunday School kids I have taught. The women I was assigned to minister to in all the different places we lived in. My kids. My kids' friends. My seminary students. Bundles of people.

As I think back over all those people I have met as we moved "from place to place, and from city to city" (D&C 79:1), my heart is also glad. Those are some of my best memories, my fondest days—days when I proclaimed "glad tidings of great joy, even the everlasting gospel," days when the Comforter taught me truth and showed me the way to go (D&C 79:1–2).

Perhaps that is the harvest of our lives, this looking back over the bundles of people we have been led to by the Lord. As we think back over that harvest, I can't help but imagine the Lord whispering to us with a smile, "Let your heart be glad" (D&C 79:4). —EBF

Reflect and Respond

Take a minute to consider your own harvest. Who are the bundles of people the Lord has led you to minister to?

Your favorite scripture in Section 79

DOCTRINE AND COVENANTS 80:3

Wherefore, **go ye and preach my gospel**, whether
to the north or to the south, to the east or to the west,
it mattereth not, for ye cannot go amiss.

I spent several years teaching seminary, which means I ended up in a lot of living rooms crowded with excited friends and family members when a missionary opened a mission call. One particular year, while we were pushing pins into a map hung in the classroom—making guesses where one of our class members might be assigned to serve—someone asked him where he hoped he would get a chance to serve. He answered, "I don't really care, but I just hope my face doesn't show any disappointment if I don't get called somewhere cool." Everyone laughed, knowing that wasn't the "right" answer but also knowing that it was the most honest answer he could give. His honesty sparked a conversation that actually led to us reading together this particular revelation that the Lord gave to Stephen Burnett.

Stephen was a teenager when he joined the Church, and he was still a teenager when he was called to preach the gospel. We loved that, in his particular case, it didn't matter to the Lord where Stephen went on his mission. Of course, all people matter to the Lord, and sometimes He has purposes in sending missionaries to particular places, but Stephen's mission call taught us what the Lord saw as important—his commission to preach the gospel. Wherever he walked, he would discover a soul that was precious in the eyes of the Lord. We decided that when we gathered for this boy's mission-call opening that night, we would cheer right when he announced his calling as a missionary rather than waiting to hear where his assignment would be. His call to preach was the celebration, not the location he would preach in. It didn't matter where he would serve, what mattered most was that he actually would. —DB

Reflect and Respond

Consider something you have been called to recently—either personally or officially in the Church. Which parts matter not?

Your favorite
scripture in
Section 80

DOCTRINE AND COVENANTS 81:4

. . . the greatest good . . .

What is the greatest good you have done in the work of the Church lately?

It might surprise you that this revelation was given as direction to counselors in the First Presidency of the Church. It suggests that being faithful in counsel, praying, and ministering will do the greatest good. Does it interest you that those three invitations could be given to every member of the Church, regardless of what your current calling is?

The Lord follows up that counsel with a few more suggestions: "Be faithful; stand in the office which I have appointed unto you; succor the weak, lift up the hands which hang down, and strengthen the feeble knees" (D&C 81:5). This section encourages a personal inventory:

- How are you doing at being faithful?
- What are you praying for today?
- When was the last time you succored, lifted, or strengthened someone?

As I read the list, it made me wonder if I was doing the greatest good. Was I leaving deliberate space in the crazy details of my day for that great good? For faith. For prayer. For ministering. For succoring, lifting, or strengthening. It caused a lot of reflection.

What if we were to set aside some time every day for incidental ministering? Maybe it looks like a phone call during which we can take time to counsel with a friend or one of our children. Maybe it is setting aside time for more intentional prayers and meditation. Perhaps it is taking a compassionate detour, even if the rest of the day requires adjusting.

The life of Jesus Christ would suggest that the greatest good actually does come from incidental ministering. Should we give it a try? —EBF

Reflect and Respond

Consider the six invitations in section 81: faith, prayer, ministering, succoring, lifting, and strengthening. Choose one area to focus on.

Your favorite scripture in Section 81

DOCTRINE AND COVENANTS 82:14

For Zion must **increase in beauty, and in holiness.**

Joseph went to Missouri in April 1832 to meet with the leadership there. He needed to resolve some disputes that had been festering and to establish the United Firm, a merging of the mercantile stores and other businesses in Ohio and Missouri into one joint firm that could help with funding the work of the Lord as well as assist the poor and needy.

A month before any of this, Joseph and Sidney Rigdon had been torn from their homes, beaten senseless, and tarred and feathered in Ohio. Remarkably, the morning after the horrific tarring and feathering event, Joseph stood and preached forgiveness to a Sunday crowd that *included* members of the mob from the night before.

A month later, when the leaders in Ohio and Missouri met, Joseph said the scene was "solemn, impressive and delightful. During the intermission, a difficulty or hardness which had existed . . . was amicably settled, and when we came together in the afternoon, all hearts seemed to rejoice."[23]

Joseph had discovered during the inspired translation of the book of Genesis that *Zion* was the name of the ancient city of Enoch. It was called Zion because they were "of one heart and one mind, and dwelt in righteousness; and there was no poor among them" (Moses 7:18). This seemed to be the object of his focus and heart—to prepare a people who could be called the same. Forgiveness, love, and care were some of the keys that led to the creation of the ancient city Zion—and that society was a pattern for the early Saints and any other people who would want to increase in beauty and holiness as they lived the same principles. —DB

Reflect and Respond

In what ways have you seen the principles of Zion in practice? In what ways could you live them?

Your favorite scripture in

Section 82

DOCTRINE AND COVENANTS 83:1

. . . concerning women and children . . .

I love how the Lord remembers.

It is a scriptural concept we are taught beginning in the Old Testament, when the Lord remembered Rachel (see Genesis 30:22) and He also remembered Hannah (see 1 Samuel 1:19). In the Doctrine and Covenants we see this remembering again. Section 83 is entirely devoted to women and children, widows and orphans—people who needed to be remembered.

If you ever wonder how the Lord feels about women, turn to the scriptures. There are verses that speak of moments when He remembered individual women. There are stories when He spent time with them one-on-one—the woman who touched His robe, the daughter of Jairus, and even Peter's mother. A woman was the first to hold Him and witness His presence here on earth. The first person He announced His mission and ministry to was a woman at a well. On the day of the Resurrection, it was a woman who was the first to witness the risen Lord.

Yes, the Lord is mindful of women.

Section 83 is a reminder of this truth. The Lord wanted to set out laws in His Church concerning the watch care of women and children, particularly widows and orphans.

I love that the Lord remembers.

He forgets not His own. —EBF

Reflect and Respond

Can you think of a scriptural account of the Lord's tender care for a woman? What did you learn?

Your favorite scripture in Section 83

DOCTRINE AND COVENANTS 84:38-39

And he that receiveth my Father receiveth my Father's kingdom; therefore all that my Father hath shall be given unto him. And **this is according to the oath and covenant** which belongeth to the priesthood.

Evan Greene, a young, "beardless boy," was one of the small group of recently returned missionaries who sat and listened to Joseph pray and receive the remarkable revelation now called section 84. The group had just returned from the East Coast, and they were reporting on their missions when they had a chance to hear the voice of the Lord through Joseph. Evan described "the exquisite cadence of the voice in which he spoke. It was as if they beheld the face of the Lord Jesus. And they did hear his voice as He declared those sacred truths."[24]

The experience of sitting and hearing the Lord's voice seemed to go into the early morning and continued on the next day as the Lord revealed the grand purposes of missions, temples, the law of consecration, and the priesthood. Perhaps for the first time, young missionaries like Evan and maybe even more seasoned leaders were seeing how all these previously revealed principles worked in harmony to create a glorious destiny for all of God's children.

The revelation sparked those like Evan who heard it to build temples, serve mission after mission, and spread the grand promises of God to all they knew. It was important to them to know for themselves and to help others learn that the Lord had made an oath and covenant to His children that He intended on keeping. Even today we are learning more and more about how big the Lord's promises are and how available He is making them to any and all who will receive the gift. He has prepared the way, taught us the way, and helps us walk the way into His glory. —DB

Reflect and Respond

What are some truths that you have learned in your life that have taken your breath away, that have seemed almost too good to be true?

Your favorite scripture in Section 84

DOCTRINE AND COVENANTS 85:1-2

Keep a history [of] . . . their manner of life.

For some reason, record keeping became really important to Joseph Smith around this time. He had a record book containing copies of his revelations. He wanted a history of the Church and gathering recorded. He purchased a book for observations and (this is my favorite) a book for keeping his history, which was entitled, "A History of the life of Joseph Smith Jr. an account of his marvelous experience . . ."[25]

It's the account of his "marvelous experience" that intrigues me most—that was what he titled the First Vision. I'm going to start referring to it as Joseph's marvelous experience from now on.

The thought of this revelation, which counsels the leaders of the Church to begin keeping histories, is intriguing to me. I love how simple the instruction was: "Keep a history, and a general church record of all things that transpire in Zion, and of all those who consecrate properties . . . ; their manner of life, their faith, and works" (D&C 85:1–2).

It's because of those records that we see God working in the lives of the people of this generation. It makes me wonder, who is keeping a record of the workings of God in my generation? Who is recording the accounts of our marvelous experiences? Would our stories of God working in our lives be as important to our future generations as the stories of the early Saints are to us? I think that is probably true for me and for you.

Perhaps we should be more intentional about keeping a record of our manner of life, our faith, and our marvelous experiences. —EBF

Reflect and Respond

What are some of the marvelous experiences that you have had lately? Have you written them down?

Your favorite scripture in Section 85

DOCTRINE AND COVENANTS 86:6-7

But the Lord saith unto them, pluck not up the tares while the blade is yet tender.... **Let the wheat and the tares grow together** until the harvest is fully ripe.

Recently, a friend of mine made covenants with the Lord and received her temple endowment. I have known her for years. When we first met, she was not interested in the temple and was wrapped up in a life of doing things her own way. When she told me her exciting news about going to the temple, she said to me, "I bet you never thought I would be here, huh?"

While working on the inspired translation of the Bible, Joseph received this particular revelation that gave new details to the Lord's parable of the wheat and the tares. In the parable, there are angels anxious to go down to the earth and reap the fields in preparation for the Lord's Second Coming. But the Lord says to wait, not to pull up the wheat and tares quite yet. Perhaps one of the reasons is because of how similar wheat and tares look when they are young plants. Modern-day Israel has a responsibility to gather in the wheat before the Lord comes again. But how do we know who is wheat and who is tares? We don't. So the Lord instructed the angels to "let the wheat and the tares grow together until the harvest is fully ripe" (D&C 86:7). He seems to be saying, *Just wait, in case you accidentally mistake a wheat for a tare.* Like my friend.

"I bet you never thought I would be here" was another way of saying, "I bet you thought I was a tare." Luckily, it didn't matter what I thought, because the Lord told me to wait. He could have said back then, *You just wait until the harvest is ripe, because then you will have a chance to see her gathered into my covenant with the rest.* —DB

Reflect and Respond

How does this advice about the wheat and tares tutor you in your responsibility to gather people to the covenants of the Lord?

Your favorite scripture in Section 86

DOCTRINE AND COVENANTS 87:1

. . . concerning the wars that will shortly come.

In the language of a prophet, the term *shortly* is a relative one. It should perhaps be viewed from a much larger perspective than our own.

It was December 25, 1832, when Joseph Smith first prophesied about the Civil War—a war that would not begin for almost thirty more years. Joseph would be dead by the time that war started.

Do you remember the details he gave in that first revelation?

• It would begin at the rebellion of South Carolina.

• The Southern States would be divided against the Northern States.

• The slaves would rise up against their masters.

We read this today and think how visionary he was. I wonder if the people at that time wondered instead if he was crazy, especially when nothing happened *for thirty years.*

Approximately ten years later, Joseph added to that prophecy. On April 2, 1843, he said, "I prophesy . . . of the difficulties . . . in South Carolina. It may probably arise through the slave question" (D&C 130:12–13). It had been a decade, and the wars that would *shortly come,* hadn't. Do you wonder what people thought? Do you wonder if they suggested he didn't know what he was talking about? I wish I would have been among the Saints on April 12, 1861—twenty years later—when the first shot of the Civil War was fired at Fort Sumter, South Carolina.

What did they think about their prophet then?

It makes me wonder what counsel from the prophet I need to be paying more attention to right now. —EBF

Reflect and Respond

What other prophecies from modern-day prophets have been fulfilled in your lifetime? What are some prophecies we are still waiting on?

Your favorite scripture in Section 87

DOCTRINE AND COVENANTS 88:68

Therefore sanctify yourselves that your minds become single to God, **and the days will come that you shall see him;** for he will unveil his face unto you, and it shall be in his own time, and in his own way, and according to his own will.

The Lord had just given Joseph Smith a revelation on war. Now, two days later, he received this revelation, described by the Prophet as the "'olive leaf' . . . plucked from the Tree of Paradise, the Lord's message of peace to us" (D&C 88, section heading).

We live in a world of drama and distraction. War has not left the world since Joseph's prophecy of it. It has continued among nations, in relationships, and in hearts. You can read about wars on news websites or on neighborhood Facebook pages. The wars in our church communities and families can be as brutal as those fought across borders.

At the time of this revelation, there was still fighting and contention between the Saints in Missouri and the Saints in Ohio. This, among other things, prevented the Saints from focusing their hearts and attention on the glory and endowment that God was anxiously waiting to pour out upon them. I love that Joseph said he got this message from the Tree of Paradise—a tree that grows in the presence of God. It came as a hint of the promise of the good that is there. It is an invitation for the people to leave behind the mess of the temporal and enter into the presence and wholeness of the Prince of light and peace. The truths in it are powerful enough to draw people away from the gravitational pull of worldliness and to sanctify themselves to walk up God's holy mountain and into His presence to see His face. He has a promise waiting for each of us there (see D&C 88:4, 69). Happily, the promises spoken of here motivated the Saints in Ohio to begin construction on the temple—a place where these promises could be made. What will the promises motivate you and me to do? —DB

Reflect and Respond

Which promises of the Lord have the power to draw you away from distraction and drama? Which ones help you feel peace?

Your favorite scripture in Section 88

DOCTRINE AND COVENANTS 89:4

In consequence of evils and designs
which do and will **exist in the hearts of
conspiring men** in the last days . . .

Have you ever wondered exactly why the Word of Wisdom was given? Perhaps you would say it was given so we would live longer, or be healthier, or so we would learn moderation in all things. Would it surprise you to know that it was actually given "in consequence of evils and designs which do and will exist in the hearts of conspiring men in the last days" (D&C 89:4)? Every time I read that verse, I can't help but think of those conspiring men and their evil designs, and then I consider where I see them in our day.

One of the things I love most about being a member of The Church of Jesus Christ of Latter-day Saints is knowing that the Lord plans to prepare a way of safety and deliverance before me through His prophet. He will warn and forewarn. He offers protection and direction. Sometimes He adapts His principles and promises to the capacity of the weakest Saints even if it means giving them time to prepare to do His will.

It is interesting that the Word of Wisdom was not a commandment when it was first given; instead it came by revelation on February 27, 1833. After Brigham Young felt the members had had sufficient time to be taught, the revelation was accepted as a commandment by unanimous vote in 1851.[26] It is a commandment we still adhere to today. The blessings of the Word of Wisdom include longer life spans, healthier people, wisdom, and a community of Saints who understand the importance of submission, abstinence, and moderation. But there is more. This commandment has offered protection to the members of the Church—safety from the evil designs of conspiring men in the last days.

A principle with a promise.

"A Word of Wisdom, for the benefit of . . . the church" (D&C 89:1). —EBF

Reflect and Respond
How has keeping the Word of Wisdom made a difference in your life?

Your favorite
scripture in
Section 89

DOCTRINE AND COVENANTS 90:28, 31

It is my will that my handmaid Vienna Jaques
...may settle down in peace.

I wonder if Vienna Jaques thought of the Lord's promise of peace as she knelt in the muddy streets of Independence in the shadow of a vicious mob. One of only two women mentioned by name in the Doctrine and Covenants, Vienna was a wealthy single woman living in one of her two homes on the East Coast when she first met the missionaries in 1831. She proved to be as faithful as she was financially successful. In her early days as a member, together with Samuel Smith and Orson Hyde, she helped establish a small branch of the Church in Boston, housing missionaries, funding the work, and gathering her network of friends to be taught the gospel. She eventually moved to Kirtland, Ohio, during an extremely difficult time financially for the Church, where she helped buy the land for the Kirtland Temple. Joseph said of her that she "proved a savior of life as pertaining to [the Church's] pecuniary concern." She is mentioned in this revelation because of her call to move to Zion. She moved to Missouri, then to Nauvoo, and finally went with the Saints to Utah, where she lived to the old age of ninety-six and eventually settled down in peace as promised.

In this revelation, the Lord established the First Presidency with counselors who hold the keys of the kingdom. The kingdom of God does have its organization functions, but at its core it is people—the family of God. It is no surprise that in the same revelation in which the Lord set up what some might consider the high quorums of the Church, He also called His handmaid Vienna Jaques by name to the same work—building up the kingdom of God in her own way.[27] —DB

Reflect and Respond

Has there been a moment in your life when you felt God called you by name?

Your favorite
scripture in
Section 90

DOCTRINE AND COVENANTS 91:4

. . . for the Spirit manifesteth truth.

When Joseph read James 1:5, the verse we are so familiar with in the New Testament, he would most likely have been reading from a Bible that included the Apocrypha, which was common for that time. The version of the Bible we use today no longer contains the Apocrypha, so when most of us read section 91, we might wonder what the Apocrypha is.

The Bible Dictionary teaches that the Apocrypha is a group of sacred books of the Jewish people that were not included in the Bible. Regarded as useful reading, the books are mostly correct, but the Lord tells Joseph they are also filled with many interpolations by man (see D&C 91:2). Some of the books in the Apocrypha included Esdras, Tobit, and some missing chapters from the book of Esther. Some of the stories appear to be fictional, while others are historical, including the history of the Maccabees, which teaches the story commemorated today in Hanukkah celebrations.

The Lord told Joseph that it wasn't needful to translate the Apocrypha, but that if someone chose to read it, it would be important to read it with the Spirit in order to benefit from it. This is important information for learning of any kind. As we read with the Spirit, truth can be made manifest, and, just as the Lord told Joseph, "Whoso is enlightened by the Spirit shall obtain benefit therefrom" (D&C 91:5).

It is advice worth taking. Next time you turn to the scriptures, ask for the Spirit to help you understand the truths you are reading. It is what Joseph would have done when he turned to that first chapter of James. When we do that, we will benefit every time. —EBF

Reflect and Respond

Has there been a time when the Spirit enlightened your understanding as you read the scriptures? What did you learn?

Your favorite scripture in Section 91

DOCTRINE AND COVENANTS 92:2

You shall be a lively member . . .

I got a text one night from a good friend who said to me, "It is so thrilling to do life together." Do you have people like that in your life—family members, friends, and neighbors who just make life bearable in the hard seasons and exciting in the others? I remember, while serving as a bishop, thinking to myself that I could never, ever do this with the same amount of happiness if I weren't serving together with the people surrounding me. I can picture the faces of several people right now who come to mind when I read the phrase "lively member" in this section of the Doctrine and Covenants.

This particular section contains advice given to a man named Frederick G. Williams. Missionaries found Dr. Williams, and it didn't take long before he was a close friend, physician, sermon writer, and support to Joseph Smith and his family. Joseph once said of him, "Brother Frederick G. Williams is one of those men in whom I place the greatest confidence and trust, for I have found him ever full of love and brotherly kindness. He is not a man of many words, but is ever winning, because of his constant mind. He shall ever have place in my heart."[28]

Joseph and Emma appreciated this man so much, they named one of their sons after him. When the Lord gave him this calling in this revelation to serve in the United Firm, He gave it with the advice to be a "lively member." To make a difference. To be ever faithful. To breathe life into the service and to the people he served with. It seems advice that he took to heart. He became someone whom Joseph may have thought was so thrilling to do life with. —DB

Reflect and Respond

Who are some people you know who serve and love as "lively members"?

Your favorite scripture in **Section 92**

DOCTRINE AND COVENANTS 93:13

. . . until he received a fulness.

The word *fulness* is repeated fifteen times in this section.

It is a section filled with descriptions of light, truth, grace, and joy. But it isn't meant to overwhelm; it describes a process of growing a little at a time.

Many years ago, I had a friend who struggled with an addiction. During one particularly tough time, I remember talking about the situation with a counselor. I was so frustrated with how things were going. It seemed like we weren't making any progress, and I wondered if my friend would ever get better. The counselor taught me a principle I have never forgotten. "You are trying to get your friend all the way up the staircase," he pointed out to me. "What if the Lord just wants you to help get your friend up one stair?" I immediately saw where my frustration was coming from: I wasn't giving my friend time for the growing process. I wanted to see the end result right then.

We have to remember that not even Jesus received a fulness at the first. He had to grow grace for grace. It took time. There was a process. The Lord gave us this process and commandments and instructions so we would know how to worship and what to worship so that we would come unto the Father in His name, "and in due time receive of his fulness" (D&C 93:19).

The Hebrew translation for the word *fulness* can mean "all that is" and "multitude." The Greek translation speaks of "completion" and "what fills." Sometimes we describe this word as meaning all that the Father has, or all that the Father is. We have been promised that one day His fulness will be ours. It is something to look forward to. But today, we just have to worry about getting up one stair. —EBF

Reflect and Respond

Which of the verses on fulness in this chapter was the most enlightening to you? Why?

Your favorite scripture in Section 93

DOCTRINE AND COVENANTS 94:12

And this house shall be **wholly dedicated unto the Lord from the foundation thereof**, for the work...

I have zero sense of direction. It is a curse. When I turned sixteen, I didn't know how to get to our local grocery store—even though we had been going there my whole life. I have other strengths, direction is just not one of them. When I moved to Utah, I discovered something about the street systems in some of the cities here that was different from the street system I grew up with. They all were numbered. And the numbers went in order. There was 100 South, then 200 South, then 300, 400, 500. It was as if this city had been built for me. What I later discovered was that the streets were numbered in some places based on the location of the temple. If I was on 7200 South, it meant that I was 72 blocks south of the temple—the center point of the city.

The word *temple* comes from the same source as *template,* which is another word for a pattern—a word that shows up in this particular revelation. The Lord was giving a pattern for the construction of the temple and other buildings in Kirtland and in Missouri. The temple was to be in the center. There is also a pattern lesson in the instruction about the printing house: it is to be "wholly dedicated unto the Lord from the foundation." When I read that, it makes me ask if I am living according to that same pattern. Am I wholly dedicated to the Lord, or just partially? Am I true to Him deep down in my foundations, or could my relationship and dedication to Him be described as parts or portions? What is at the center of my life? As the early Saints built temples and printing houses according to these patterns, I wonder if they discovered the Lord was building them as people according to the same ones. —DB

Reflect and Respond

Have you ever met people you would describe as "wholly dedicated" or centered upon the Lord? What could you learn from them?

Your favorite scripture in Section 94

DOCTRINE AND COVENANTS 95:8

I gave unto you a commandment that
you should build a house.

In 1833, when this revelation was given, the Saints were gathering in two separate locations: Kirtland, Ohio, and Jackson County, Missouri. If you haven't been to either of those locations, it can be hard to understand what was happening. Last fall, on a tour of Church history sites, we drove from Pennsylvania to New York and then to Ohio and walked through each of the sites. However, when we traveled from Kirtland, Ohio, to Jackson County, Missouri, we flew on an airplane across four states and then drove by bus the rest of the way. In Joseph's day, it took five to seven days for the Saints to travel between the two places.

The Saints in Kirtland were terribly poor. They were gathering in more and more people daily, trying to make do with what they had. The Saints in Missouri were struggling with intense persecution and mobs, but there was also fighting within the Church that was preventing them from moving forward with what the Lord had asked.

At this time, the Lord gave similar commandments to both groups: "Build a house, in the which house I design to endow those whom I have chosen with power from on high" (D&C 95:8). The commandment had been given to both groups, and both groups were struggling to fulfill it. It would require great sacrifice for a people who were already feeling the pain of sacrifice.

Section 95 is a chastening because of the failure to build those houses. God knew the protection that would come from those temples. The gifts. The promises. The understanding. But the Saints would have to trust that their sacrifice would lead to His promise. —EBF

Reflect and Respond

Has the Lord ever asked you to do something that didn't make sense? Did you receive a blessing because of it?

Your favorite
scripture in
Section 95

DOCTRINE AND COVENANTS 96:6

It is wisdom and expedient in me, that my servant John Johnson
whose offering I have accepted, and whose prayers I have
heard, unto whom I give a promise of eternal life . . .

My grandmother's best friend invited her to girls camp the year she moved from California to Ogden. That began a domino effect of faith that has not ended. She was able to attend my daughter's (her great-granddaughter's) baptism last year. So much good has come from the simple sacrifice and invitation of one willing soul.

I suppose all of us have stories like this, whether we know about them or not. Most of the good in our lives, if not all, hinges on the goodness of others. For those who find sacred strength in the keys restored in the Kirtland Temple—keys for temple ordinances, keys to seal husbands and wives, keys to seal children to parents, and so on and so on—for those who have experienced sanctification from these events, we have John Johnson, in part, to thank for that.

The early leaders in Kirtland were looking for land on which to build the Kirtland Temple and found a farm owned by a settler named Peter French. When he agreed to sell the land, the Saints agreed to buy it in obedience to the Lord's commandments and in anticipation of the good things to come. Unfortunately, they didn't have the funds. Fortunately, they had John Johnson. John and his wife, Alice, joined the Church in 1831, during the time the Saints were moving into the Kirtland area. Joseph and Emma actually lived at their home for a while, and in the summer of 1833 John sacrificed again to give place for the Lord to have a home. He sold his own farm and gave the money to pay for a large portion of the cost of the land where the Kirtland Temple would later be built.[29] That is the offering the Lord accepted—except it wasn't just money, it was his heart. And the goodness from that sacrifice has been ongoing ever since. —DB

Reflect and Respond

Describe a time when you felt your offering (no matter how small) was accepted by the Lord.

Your favorite
scripture in
Section 96

DOCTRINE AND COVENANTS 97:27

I, the Lord, have accepted of her offering.

By the time this revelation came, the Saints had been forced to sign an agreement to leave Jackson County. They hadn't built the temple. The foretold gathering had not taken place. The center of Zion hadn't been established. Their lives hadn't been perfect. They had struggled against human nature both within and outside of the Church. They hadn't accomplished all that the Lord had asked them to do.

Maybe you have felt some of those same feelings.

I had the sacred opportunity of helping to keep watch over a friend as she prepared to leave mortality and return to her heavenly home. Our conversations over the course of those last few days were sacred. I don't know if I have ever met a more stalwart woman, and yet, the conversation I remember most was her concern that she hadn't done all that had been asked of her, that the Lord would not be satisfied with what she had done with her life. Every time she spoke of it, it brought her to tears.

When she died, her family asked if I would speak at her funeral. As I was preparing my talk, I stumbled on these verses that the Lord spoke over His Saints as they prepared to leave behind what was unfinished in Missouri: "Nevertheless, let it be read this once to her ears, that I, the Lord, have accepted of her offering; . . . and I will bless her with blessings, and multiply a multiplicity of blessings upon her, and upon her generations forever and ever" (D&C 97:27–28).

It was impressed upon me that all the Lord asks of us is our best, whatever that may be. He sees our frustrations and our inadequacies and our struggles. And still, He accepts our offering, and He plans to continue to bless us no matter where we are. —EBF

Reflect and Respond

How does it make you feel to know that all the Lord asks of you is your best on that day, whatever that best might be?

Your favorite scripture in Section 97

DOCTRINE AND COVENANTS 98:1

Verily I say unto you my friends, fear not, **let your hearts be comforted**; yea, rejoice evermore, and in everything give thanks.

Jackson County was under attack, and word of the disasters may have already reached Joseph by the time he received this revelation, but most historians agree[30] he could not have known the extent of the horrors the Saints in Missouri were facing at the hands of angry mobs. Their leaders were beaten, tarred, and feathered; their houses were ransacked; their printing press—which they had purchased at such great sacrifice—was destroyed; and they were driven from their homes. The inspired advice and comforting tenderness that was delivered to the Saints in this revelation must have come as a welcome gift in a very troubled time.

I always imagine that they read and talked about the revelations over and over, looking for any sort of answer or reprieve the Lord could give. Of all the promises and counsel in this revelation, the one I think I would have treasured the most came at the very beginning: "Fear not."

Fear not is a phrase often used by angels in the scriptures (see Luke 1:13, 30; 2:10). It is a command that comes from heaven—and when heaven knows what you are facing and tells you not to fear, you can take courage. But the Lord also knows how easy it is to fear, especially in a situation like the one the Saints were in. That is why I love the word *let* in the next sentence, "Let your hearts be comforted." It is almost as if He is saying: It will not feel natural to be comforted during the trouble you are facing. Fear will come again and again. So, *let* your heart be comforted. Allow it to happen. Choose to believe in heaven. Choose to believe in God. —DB

Reflect and Respond

What advice would you give others who are trying to learn how to let their hearts be comforted?

Your favorite scripture in Section 98

DOCTRINE AND COVENANTS 99:1

**. . . from house to house, from village
to village, and from city to city . . .**

Do you remember John Murdock? He was the man whose wife died in childbirth after she delivered twins. He gave the twins to Emma and Joseph to raise. In section 99, a little over one year after losing his wife, John was called on a mission. His call was to go from house to house, from village to village, and from city to city and declare the word.

In the midst of a devastating trial, the Lord gave John a place to serve—a cause to be devoted to. Something to keep him going.

Many years ago, I became very ill. I couldn't get out of bed for months. At the time, I had been called to serve as an early-morning seminary teacher in my stake. When I was set apart, I was given a promise that I would be resilient for the entire time I had the calling. As sick as I was that year, I rarely missed teaching that class. I would wake up early in the morning, get dressed, go and teach, and then return home and climb into bed for the rest of the day. That class gave my life purpose and direction in a time of devastation and disappointment. I didn't go from house to house or village to village, but I did drive to the stake center every morning and prepare to teach, and my life was blessed because of it.

John Murdock's call would last only a few years. The same was true for me. But I held onto the promise I had been given that, for as long as I served, I would reap blessings, and I recognized those blessings throughout those years.

Sometimes healing comes through the process of a journey, through giving our heart to something else for a time. It was true for John Murdock, and the same will be true for each of us. If you are in the midst of difficulty or heartache, allow the Lord to take you on a journey—from village to village. Invest your heart in the work. Healing will come. —EBF

Reflect and Respond

*Has there been a time when healing has come as you devoted yourself
to the Lord's work? What did you learn from that experience?*

Your favorite
scripture in
Section 99

DOCTRINE AND COVENANTS 100:1

Your families are well; **they are in mine hands,** and
I will do with them as seemeth me good.

Six months after Freeman and Huldah Nickerson were baptized into the restored Church, they went to Kirtland to visit Joseph Smith to request that he and some other elders come up to their home in Canada to preach the gospel to their family.[31] They had found a thrill in hearing the message and entering into covenants, and they now wanted their families to hear and have a chance to experience the same beauty. When Joseph and others agreed to go, several members in Kirtland came with requests that the Prophet stop on his way to visit some of their loved ones as well.

This is a common pattern found throughout scripture: someone feels the redemptive grace of the gospel and then immediately wishes it for others. This same love was manifested by Joseph while he was on this mission. At the time, he was twenty-seven years old and had two young children at home. A gentleman who had joined the Church had recently turned against it and was stirring up persecution against the members of the Church, in particular Joseph and his family. On top of it, the news of the city of Zion being ransacked and the potential trouble there weighed heavily on Joseph. He spent many nights praying for his family and the Saints he loved so much—those back home and the ones he was meeting on his mission.

On one particularly anxious day, Joseph prayed and was promised in this revelation that all those he loved were in God's hands. For those he would preach to, He was promised words "in the very moment" he needed them (D&C 100:6). This seems to be another pattern in scripture. God is in charge, and He will fulfill all His promises. We might not know when or how, but blessings will be given in the moment we need them. —DB

Reflect and Respond

What are your prayers for your family members right now? What evidence do you see of the Lord holding them in His hands?

Your favorite
scripture in
Section 100

DOCTRINE AND COVENANTS 101:16

Be still and know that I am God.

The mob in Jackson County continued persecuting the Saints until all members of the Church were driven out of the county. Most of the Saints fled north, where they had to cross the Missouri River. The shores of the river near the ferry were lined with refugees. Some people were fortunate enough to escape with some of their household goods, but many lost everything. Parley P. Pratt wrote: "Hundreds of people were seen in every direction, some in tents and some in the open air around their fires, while the rain descended in torrents. Husbands were inquiring for their wives, wives for their husbands; parents for children, and children for parents. . . . The scene was indescribable, and, I am sure, would have melted the hearts of any people on the earth, except our blind oppressors, and a blind and ignorant community."[32]

In the first two verses of this section the Lord tells Joseph He allowed the affliction to come upon the Saints in consequence of their transgressions, but the Lord promised He wouldn't walk away from the Saints. He might be slow to answer their prayers, but He would listen. At the end of the section, the Lord promises that there will come a time when the Saints will dwell on that land. A time when they will build, and no one will take away their houses, and they will plant and be blessed to eat the fruit. A time of safety and not running away, a time of abundance without fear of loss.

I wonder how many of them carried that one sentence of promise with them in their hearts, "Be still and know that I am God" (D&C 101:16). There would be more than a trail of bloody feet and blankets soaked through with rain. There would be houses and gardens and peace. God had promised, and He would provide. —EBF

Reflect and Respond
Sometimes chastening and suffering turn our hearts to the Lord. When have you experienced a sanctifying moment like this?

Your favorite scripture in
Section 101

DOCTRINE AND COVENANTS 102:14

But **if it is thought to be difficult,** four shall be
appointed; and if more difficult, six . . .

A friend of mine recently asked if I had any advice for her in her new calling to serve as a Relief Society president. I had never been one before, and I don't think I ever will be, but I had recently been released as a bishop, so she was trying to get advice from that angle. She didn't need any advice from me, but the first thing I wanted to say to her was to *speak up.* I told her that when, as a bishop, I had extended callings to presidents of organizations, I would first call them to the ward council, and then second as president of the organization. Some might disagree with the order, but I did it to emphasize something very important to me: I wanted them all to know that they were going to come to those council meetings as active participants, not just representatives of their organizations.

When Joseph organized a high council in Kirtland (about a year before the Quorum of the Twelve was organized), he told the elders there that he "would show the order of councils in ancient days as shown to him by vision."[33] The principle of councils is not new, and the Lord has been using groups as a means of sending revelation to the world since ancient times. The Lord gave beautiful principles to Joseph in this revelation about counseling in councils, but one of my favorites is found in verse 14, about gathering more when situations are difficult. There is strength in numbers. There is power in collective wisdom. There are promises when "two or three are gathered together" in His name (D&C 6:32). If a matter is difficult, gather people to help; if it is more difficult, gather more. Ours is a God of gathering in, a Counsellor who believes in the power of councils. —DB

Reflect and Respond
What have you learned about the wisdom of gathering councils?

Your favorite
scripture in
Section 102

DOCTRINE AND COVENANTS 103:15

The redemption of Zion
must needs come by power . . .

When Joseph heard the counsel from the Lord to redeem Zion with power, he immediately gathered an army to right the wrong in Jackson County. Zion's Camp became the name of this group. By the time they were ready to leave, the group consisted of 207 men, 11 women, and 11 children.

It took two months for them to march to Missouri. When they got close, the governor sent word telling them not to come because he would not provide help. It would not be too many days before the army would give up their pursuit and return home.[34]

As you read, you can't help but wonder why. Why did the Lord not fight that battle for the Saints? Why wasn't Zion redeemed? Where was the promised power of the Lord?

It isn't until section 105 that we find out part of the answer: "This cannot be brought to pass until mine elders are endowed with power from on high" (D&C 105:11). Suddenly everything becomes clear: the power the Lord is talking about isn't an army, it's an endowment. The redemption of Zion would have to wait a little season, until the people of the Church had been endowed with power—the power that would redeem Zion.

"Zion's Camp . . . had furnished the know-how and experience which made possible the subsequent exodus of more than 20,000 men, women, and children from Nauvoo to the Rocky Mountains, and prepared leaders for the great exodus. It also provided a proving ground—some 1,000 miles of it—for the future Church leaders. . . . When the Quorum of the Twelve Apostles was 'searched out' . . . most of those chosen had been members of Zion's Camp. These men had demonstrated their willingness to sacrifice everything, even life itself, when commanded by the Lord."[35] —EBF

Reflect and Respond

Why do you think waiting for an endowment of power was crucial to the redemption of Zion?

Your favorite
scripture in
Section 103

DOCTRINE AND COVENANTS 104:80

Behold**, I will soften the hearts** of those to whom you are in debt, until I shall send means unto you for your deliverance.

When the mobs destroyed the store and printing press in Missouri, a heavy financial debt fell on the Kirtland Saints. Tragically, they were having their own money troubles in Ohio. They owed money on the temple lot and money for goods they bought for the store. Joseph could not raise enough even to visit the Saints in Jackson County, much less resume the printing of the revelations. The Church and its leaders were drowning in debt and on the brink of financial ruin when John Tanner received an impression by dream or vision "that he . . . must go immediately to the Church"[36] in Kirtland. And that's exactly what he did, in January 1835.

Six months before, the Lord had counseled Church leaders to find ways to raise money to pay debts. In the end of that particular revelation came this promise of deliverance: "I will soften the hearts . . . I shall send means . . ." (D&C 104:80). That deliverance came on a wagon, six months later, in January 1835—right in the nick of time. "Brother Joseph, you are welcome to it," were the words John Tanner said to the Prophet when Joseph approached him with a promissory note for the $2,000 that John had lent to the Church to build the Kirtland Temple. "Keep it," was what John essentially said to Joseph. "You don't need to pay me back."

John Tanner rescued the finances of the Church within days of its falling into serious trouble. It makes me wonder, in the middle of my troublesome places, what hearts God is softening and what means He is sending for deliverance for me. —DB

Reflect and Respond
When has God been a God of deliverance for you?

Your favorite scripture in Section 104

DOCTRINE AND COVENANTS 105:40

All things shall work together for your good.

It must have been frustrating when the Lord said, "wait," after the Saints had gathered their 200 men, after they had walked the two-month journey, after all the hardship and suffering. It was especially hard because the end goal was in sight. It was so reachable. All they had to do was cross the river. But the Lord said, "wait." The Lord of hosts. The Lord of David who killed Goliath. The Lord of the angel armies who stood on the mountain when Elijah escaped. The Lord who parted the Red Sea and then swallowed up the army of Egyptians. That same Lord said, "wait for a little season" (D&C 105:13). Why?

This section tells us it was because He had prepared a blessing and an endowment. He had accepted their offering. The men who were in this army just needed to experience a trial of their faith. It wasn't required of them to fight. The losing of their lives in that battle was a spiritual commitment, not a physical one.

Zion's Camp raised up the strength of His house, even His warriors, the young men and the middle-aged. But it wasn't time to fight. First the army had to become very great, and they had to become sanctified. Then the Lord would fight their battles.

It had been a day of calling, and now would come a day of choosing. He would choose those who were worthy from that army. They would lead the Church. They would gather the Saints. They would prepare for the redemption of Zion—and all things would work together for their good (see D&C 105:40). I love how the Lord reminded them, right there on the side of that river, the place where they would turn around and walk back home, that all things would work together for their good. Even this. —EBF

Reflect and Respond

Has there been a time when the Lord has told you to wait for a little while? What did you learn in that season?

Your favorite scripture in Section 105

DOCTRINE AND COVENANTS 106:8

And I will give him **grace and assurance** wherewith he may stand.

I can remember a few times in my life sitting in my bed, looking up at the ceiling, and wondering, "What in the world have I gotten myself into?" The first time I remember feeling that way was on my first night in the MTC. "I can't be a representative of the Lord! He is THE LORD! And I am me." I thought it again when I became a father for the first time. "How did God trust me with this little one?" I thought it again when my second baby came. And then again, and again, and again, and again (was that six?).

I have felt it with other callings and other promptings as well. I wonder sometimes if Warren Cowdery felt the same thing after he was called to be a presiding high priest over his branch in New York after having been baptized only a few months earlier. He was Oliver's older brother, and you might remember that he was initially supposed to board with the Smiths back in 1829 as a teacher but couldn't take the position, which was why Oliver went in his place and there first learned about the gold plates. Warren lived back in upstate New York, and because of the sympathy he felt for the Saints in Missouri, he opened his home to Joseph Smith and others when they came recruiting members to join Zion's Camp.[37] Warren was baptized a few months later, in 1834, and soon after that wrote a letter to Oliver requesting that someone come and lead the little congregation that he belonged to in Freedom, New York. The answer came as this revelation, in which the Lord called Warren himself to be that leader. I have taken comfort from the Lord's promise to Warren that He would give him both grace and assurance to stand in the position he was called to. He would need it. And so have I. —DB

Reflect and Respond

What is the difference between grace and assurance, and what is the benefit of the promise of both from the Lord?

Your favorite scripture in Section 106

DOCTRINE AND COVENANTS 107:31

The promise is . . .

When I read section 107, I focus less on learning about the details of the two priesthoods, and more on learning the character of the Father.

I discover how the Father carefully prepared the details of the priesthood so that His earthly family would have order. He provided a system of confidence, faith, and prayer. Special witnesses. Leaders who would be called and set apart and ordained unto this power. The ability to administer in spiritual things and in the outward ordinances. A people who would be watched over by quorums who served "in all righteousness, in holiness, and lowliness of heart, meekness and long suffering, and in faith, and virtue, and knowledge, temperance, patience, godliness, brotherly kindness and charity" (D&C 107:30).

I read those words and realize that verse is a description of the Father. It makes me pause to study every word individually, because I long to know more about the Father.

This is the verse that follows: "Because the promise is, if these things abound in them they shall not be unfruitful in the knowledge of the Lord" (D&C 107:31). The more we come to understand and acquire those characteristics, the more we will know and understand the Father— because we will be like Him.

It was a priesthood order handed down from father to son. *From Father.* An order that would help us become like Him. We would "have the privilege of receiving the mysteries of the kingdom of heaven, to have the heavens opened unto them, to commune with the general assembly and church of the Firstborn, and to enjoy the communion and presence of God the Father, and Jesus the mediator of the new covenant" (D&C 107:19). It is a blessing promised to every covenant keeper in the Church. How great is our privilege! —EBF

Reflect and Respond

How have the ordinances of the gospel helped you know more about the character of God?

Your favorite scripture in Section 107

DOCTRINE AND COVENANTS 108:2

**Let your soul be at rest concerning
your spiritual standing.**

I was once in a question-and-answer session of stake conference when a sister stood and asked, "How can I know if I am doing enough to make it?" My heart groaned when I heard the anxiety in her voice. There she was—a faithful Saint at a stake conference meeting wondering about her salvation. Perhaps she was inspired to ask about it.

Lyman Sherman, a man whom many don't know, once received an impression from the Lord to go to Joseph and ask him for further direction. And so he did, and by the end of the day, Joseph had received this particular revelation for him.[38] If I were in Lyman's shoes, I would be intrigued by two bits of counsel that came. The first is this sweet assurance from the Lord about Lyman's spiritual standing. It makes me think that maybe he was asking himself questions similar to this sister at stake conference. "Let your soul be at rest." The next bit of advice surprised me at first. "Arise up and be more careful henceforth in observing your vows" (D&C 108:3). When I read them one after the other, I learn a powerful pair of principles from Lyman's revelation. His spiritual standing can be right with the Lord at the same time that he needs counsel and direction. The Lord can be pleased with him *while* he is falling short. Lyman hadn't "made it" to becoming the person he wanted to be yet, but that didn't mean he needed to be anxious. The Lord wanted him to rest—rest in what He, Jesus, had done to rescue Lyman—while at the same time seeking to become someone better.

I can't remember how the stake president answered that one sister that night, but if she came seeking, perhaps the Lord would say to her something similar to what He said to Lyman. I think He would. —DB

Reflect and Respond

How would you answer and counsel this sister if you had a chance to talk with her?

Your favorite
scripture in
Section 108

DOCTRINE AND COVENANTS 109:5

**Out of our poverty we have
given of our substance.**

This is such a beautiful description of the word *sacrifice*—a giving of substance out of a place of poverty. I wonder, what would that look like for you?

It was a time of great poverty when the Saints sacrificed so greatly to build a house they would soon walk away from. They did it for two reasons: first, so the Lord would "have a place to manifest himself to his people," and second, "to secure a fulfilment of the promises" God had made to His people (see D&C 109:5, 11). From that sacrifice came a host of blessings that were promised to those who would attend the temple they had sacrificed for. Here are just a few:

They may feel His power
Be taught words of wisdom
Grow up unto Him
Receive a fulness of the
   Holy Ghost
Be organized
Become prepared
They may speedily repent
Find favor in His sight
Be restored to His blessings
Be armed with power
Have His name upon them

Have His glory round about
Angels have charge over
   them
May bear great tidings
Know this is my work
He will put forth His hand
Be established
No weapon will prosper
Wickedness shall not have
   power
He will fight for His people
They may be delivered

Receive a testimony of
   covenant
Prepare the hearts
May not faint in trouble
Thy grace assisting them
Delivered
Be enabled
We will be remembered
Become pure
Become righteous
Receive glory
Reap joy

I love that it was written for the children of Jacob, "who have been scattered upon the mountains for a long time, in a cloudy and dark day" (D&C 109:61), because I have had cloudy and dark days. On those days I want to remember this list of blessings. —EBF

Reflect and Respond

What sacrifices do you make to attend the temple? What blessings have you recognized?

Your favorite
scripture in
Section 109

DOCTRINE AND COVENANTS 110:10

This is **the beginning of the blessing . . .**

People who see or visit the Kirtland Temple today might be a little underwhelmed. If you compare it to some of the magnificent and palatial temples dotting the earth today, it doesn't look very impressive. But when you consider the poverty level of the Church members when they built it, and you hear stories of those who gave everything to see it rise, it becomes a testament of some of the most impressive sacrifices in our history, and immediately it becomes beautiful.

Section 110 is an account of another reason you might be in awe of the first temple built in our dispensation. About a week after the dedication, Joseph and Oliver were kneeling behind curtains that hung to divide sections of the Kirtland Temple and were visited by four heavenly personages. The first was Jesus, the Lord and Savior, who crowned the temple with His presence and personally accepted the sacrificial gift. Following His visit, other heavenly messengers came bestowing keys upon the Prophet. Those keys would open the door to blessings the Saints had previously not enjoyed—blessings that families are still immersed in today. The temple was dedicated in 1836, and the keys to seal couples and families and to save our deceased ancestors have continued since that day.

I once went to the temple baptistry in Houston, Texas, with a convert friend who was standing in the font for his two grandfathers. After his baptism, still dripping wet, he sat in a chair by the font and was confirmed for them as well. The Spirit was poured out in that room that evening, just as it was in another temple back in 1836. That experience has been repeated again and again all over the world. Truly, April 3, 1836, was just the beginning of great blessings. —DB

Reflect and Respond
What blessed experiences and gifts in your life can you trace back to the keys received on April 3, 1836?

Your favorite scripture in Section 110

DOCTRINE AND COVENANTS 111:10

For there are **more treasures
than one** for you in this city.

The trip that Joseph took to Salem, Massachusetts, in the summer of 1836 was not the first one in his lifetime. He had gone there when he was just seven years old to live with his uncle while he recovered from his leg operation. This time he went for a different purpose. Even though everyone was excited about the newly finished temple, the Church was still heavily in debt, and poor Saints were moving to Kirtland in a steady flow, hoping the Church would be able to assist them financially. During this time of financial desperation, a gentleman named William Burgess came to Joseph claiming there was Spanish treasure buried in Salem that only he knew the location of. The Prophet was persuaded, and he, Sidney, Hyrum, and Oliver all set out for the East Coast to handle some business and hopefully find some treasure that could help with their debts. Unfortunately, when they got there, William could not find the treasure. Despite a lot of searching, the trip to Salem came up empty.

The story brings up so many questions, and even though the revelation Joseph received in Salem doesn't answer all of them, it teaches several principles perhaps more valuable than the Spanish gold. The Lord told Joseph He wasn't mad at him for making the trip, even though He considered it a folly (see D&C 111:1). He then promised him treasure of another kind in that city. Some of that treasure would be the knowledge they gained while they were there, but another treasure would be people. Years later, Hyrum gave Erastus Snow, an Apostle, a copy of the revelation and sent him to Salem to fulfill it—which he did by baptizing a small branch of 120 souls. It seems as if God can turn our follies into treasure after all. —DB

Reflect and Respond

When has God turned a mistake into a treasured detour or new experience for you?

Your favorite scripture in Section 111

DOCTRINE AND COVENANTS 112:10

Be thou humble . . .

Thomas Marsh was an Apostle, the President of the Quorum of the Twelve. He was tasked with trying to repair the infighting, to settle the unrest among Church members. He knew things were bad, but when his wife bought a cow to share with a friend, things got worse. They were supposed to exchange milk and strippings each week so they would have enough cream to make cheese. But without telling her friend, Mrs. Marsh kept an extra pint every week so she could make extra. There was a Church trial, and Mrs. Marsh was found guilty of defrauding her friend.

Thomas had been given a warning in section 112—contend for the Church, do not move out of Zion, be humble, love others, and do not rebel against Joseph. It was very specific counsel. But Thomas moved out of Zion, he left the Church, and he rebelled against Joseph—and he didn't do it quietly. He wrote a letter to the governor of Missouri that contributed to his issuing the extermination order against the Saints.

Years later, Thomas wanted to come back. He said, "The Lord could get along well without me . . . but, oh, what have I lost."[39]

Remember what the Lord told Thomas, "Inasmuch as they shall humble themselves before me, *and* abide in my word, *and* hearken to the voice of my Spirit" (D&C 112:22; emphasis added). Thomas forgot about those three things.

Maybe one day we will find ourselves in a similar situation, crying over spilt milk. I would say this: Don't lose the Spirit. Don't leave the prophet. Don't get mad.

Sell the cow. —EBF

....

Reflect and Respond
How could you humble yourself, abide more in His word, and listen to the voice of the Spirit?

Your favorite scripture in **Section 112**

DOCTRINE AND COVENANTS 113:8

. . . to put on the authority of the priesthood.

This revelation came because of a question from Elias Higbee, who was a judge. Joseph described him as a great and mighty man. He spent time in Washington, D.C., lobbying to Congress for the Saints. At one point he wrote a letter to the Prophet saying, "I feel now that we have made our last appeal to all earthly tribunals; that we should now put our whole trust in the God of Abraham, Isaac, and Jacob. We have a right now which we could not heretofore so fully claim—that is, of asking God for redress and redemption, as they have been refused us by man."[40]

It is that last line that catches my attention. *We have a right . . . that is, of asking God. . . .* Elias Higbee was a man who was trained to ask questions, to find answers in order to pass judgment. I love that section 113 is a section devoted to Elias Higbee's questions.

In it we learn that those whom God calls in the last days, those who hold His power to gather and to redeem, those who put upon His strength are acting in the authority of the priesthood. Called. To gather. To put upon His strength. It is my favorite definition of the authority of the priesthood.

But that is not the only lesson we learn from this section. The most important lesson we learn is that we have a right to ask God any question we have. Elias had four questions in March of 1838. I'm sure there were many more questions he asked over the span of his life. He believed in a God who would answer those questions because he believed it was his right to ask and receive those answers.

What are your questions? Where have you gone for answers? We have a right to ask God. We should. —EBF

Reflect and Respond
What is the question you would like to ask God?

Your favorite scripture in Section 113

DOCTRINE AND COVENANTS 114:2

Inasmuch as there are **those among you who deny my name, others shall be planted in their stead.**

David W. Patten might be my favorite hero of the Doctrine and Covenants. He served three missions before Joseph sent him to help the exiled Saints in Missouri. Joseph described him then as a kind angel from heaven. When he arrived in Missouri, he spent both day and night ministering to the Saints. Throughout his life, David W. Patten was one of the bravest advocates for the Church, which earned him the title "Captain Fearnot."

In October 1838, the news reached Far West that prisoners had been taken near Crooked River. Captain Fearnot responded by calling seventy-five men to serve under his command. As they approached the river a shot was fired, and a battle began. "With the watch-word 'God and Liberty' on his lips, David, ordering a charge, ran forward. The mob fled in confusion before the rush that followed. . . . As David led the pursuit down the riverbank, a mobber who had taken refuge behind a tree . . . turned and shot him in the abdomen."[41]

David Patten's dying words were, "I feel that I have kept the faith, I have finished my course, henceforth there is laid up for me a crown . . . whatever you do else, O do not deny the faith." Three years later, the Prophet was assured by the Lord, "My servant David Patten . . . is with me at this time" (D&C 124:19).

We must remember that during a time of great apostasy in the Church, some will rise to its defense. There will be people who will keep the faith and finish the course, kind angels from heaven who will fight for God and liberty. —EBF

Reflect and Respond

What can you do to be more like Captain Fearnot?

Your favorite scripture in
Section 114

DOCTRINE AND COVENANTS 115:4

For **thus shall my church be called in the last days,**
even The Church of Jesus Christ of Latter-day Saints.

Maybe you remember the general conference when President Russell M. Nelson released a statement asking the world to use the correct name of the Church. He asked us if we wondered why it was necessary or if we thought it was inconsequential. Then he reminded us that it was the Savior Himself who named the Church: "For thus shall my church be called in the last days, even The Church of Jesus Christ of Latter-day Saints" (D&C 115:4).

President Nelson reminded us that we promise to take the Lord's name each week when we take the sacrament. But there was more. It was the prophetic blessing he extended at the end of his talk that has been imprinted into my heart. "I promise you that if we will do our best to restore the correct name of the Lord's Church, He whose Church this is will pour down His power and blessings upon the heads of the Latter-day Saints, the likes of which we have never seen. We will have the knowledge and power of God to help us take the blessings of the restored gospel of Jesus Christ to every nation, kindred, tongue, and people and to prepare the world for the Second Coming of the Lord."[42]

If we do our best to remember the name of the Church, the Lord will pour down power and blessings the likes of which we have never seen. We will be able to take the gospel into every nation. We will prepare the world for the Second Coming of the Lord.

Those are not inconsequential blessings. If those blessings are what will follow our doing our best to call our Church by its correct name, then I am all in.

I can't wait to see the miracles He has in store. —EBF

Reflect and Respond

How have you implemented the prophet's counsel to use the correct name of the Church? Has it been hard for you? Why or why not?

Your favorite
scripture in
Section 115

DOCTRINE AND COVENANTS 116:1

**Spring Hill is named by
the Lord Adam-ondi-Ahman.**

I have been to Adam-ondi-Ahman several times in my life. It is one of my favorite places to visit. I love to consider what was, what is, and what is to come. Joseph Smith taught us that this is the place where Adam will come in the days leading up to the Second Coming. Because of that revelation, the Church cares for that property very carefully. If you are looking, you notice that care every time you visit that place.

Each time I have been there, I have set aside a couple hours for the visit. I love wandering through the perfectly manicured meadows and the shady groves that wait, heavy with the anticipation of good things to come. Every tree whispers of the past and stands waiting for what the future holds. The fences are painted white. The lawns are freshly mowed.

It was on my most recent visit, as I wandered under the shade of the trees overhanging the path, that I heard the Spirit whisper these words softly into my heart: *constant readiness.* I looked at those grounds and thought, *No man knows the time, and yet at Adam-ondi-Ahman everything is in constant readiness for the moment when He will return.*

I wonder, can the same be said of me?

I thought of that beautiful place waiting ready and decided I wanted to commit to that same readiness. I want to stand ready and waiting for what the future holds—looking forward with anticipation to the good things that will come. —EBF

Reflect and Respond

What principle can you learn from Adam-ondi-Ahman? How could you be more ready for the Second Coming of the Lord?

Your favorite scripture in Section 116

DOCTRINE AND COVENANTS 117:13

**His sacrifice shall be more
sacred unto me than his increase.**

There are three lessons in section 117 that cannot be overlooked as the Lord gives counsel to three separate men. Each lesson raises a question that we can learn from today.

First, as He speaks to William Marks and Newel K. Whitney, the Lord reminds them that He holds "the destinies of all. . . . Therefore, will I not make solitary places to bud and to blossom, and to bring forth in abundance?" (D&C 117:6–7). Where are the solitary places in your life? How can you strengthen your trust in the Lord and allow His Spirit to lead you to discover the abundance there?

Second, the Lord cautions Newel K. Whitney about his "littleness of soul" (D&C 117:11). It is an interesting phrase, especially as we consider the opposite of this characteristic in D&C 121:42 and Alma 32:28. What do you learn about the difference between having a littleness of soul and participating in experiences that enlarge the soul?

Third, Oliver Granger is being asked to go to Kirtland and try to settle the Church's debts there. The Saints were leaving, and time will show that Oliver would not be as successful as anyone would have hoped. I love that the Lord still sends him into a venture that will not be profitable and says to him at the beginning, "Let him contend earnestly . . . and when he falls he shall rise again, for his sacrifice shall be more sacred unto me than his increase" (D&C 117:13).

Have you ever been in a situation that has not come to fruition in the way you would have liked? Have you ever experienced failure? Does it give you courage to realize that sometimes the Lord knows we will fall even when we are contending earnestly for a good cause? What do you think it means for a sacrifice to be more sacred than an increase? —EBF

Reflect and Respond

Choose one of the three sets of questions and take some time to reflect on your own personal situation. What do you learn?

Your favorite scripture in Section 117

DOCTRINE AND COVENANTS 118:3

I, the Lord, give unto them a promise . . . **an effectual door
shall be opened for them,** from henceforth.

During a time of building up cities in Missouri, when things were relatively optimistic
and peaceful, Joseph received a revelation in July 1838 that the Quorum of the Twelve
should leave for their mission to England from the Far West Temple site in April 1839,
nine months later. Between the time of the revelation and 1839, the Saints were officially
kicked out of the state of Missouri, Joseph and others were incarcerated in Liberty Jail,
and the temple site was abandoned. Wilford Woodruff, a recent convert, who had just
been called to fill a vacancy in the Quorum of the Twelve, wrote about the time: "What
is to be done? Here is a revelation commanding the Twelve to be in Far West on the
26th day of April, to lay the corner stone of the Temple there; it had to be fulfilled. The
Missourians had sworn by all the gods of eternity that if every other revelation given
through Joseph Smith were fulfilled, that should not be, for the day and date being given
they declared that it should fail."[43]

Brigham Young insisted that the brethren follow through with the command. I think
Wilford learned something about the Lord (and Brigham's trust in Him) when he sat on
a newly laid cornerstone at the Far West Temple site and was ordained an Apostle a little
past midnight on April 26, 1839. The prophecy was fulfilled, and the quorum members
left from that spot on their missions. Once again, the Lord opened a door for them—as
He would continue to do on their mission to England and beyond. —DB

Reflect and Respond

*We hear often that God opens doors. When has He opened one for
you in a surprising way?*

Your favorite
scripture in
Section 118

DOCTRINE AND COVENANTS 119:3

This shall be **the beginning of
the tithing** of my people.

"Tithing is so simple and straightforward a thing. The principle, as it applies to us, is actually set forth in one verse of section 119 of the Doctrine and Covenants.

"'And after that [after the Saints offered their 'surplus property' to the bishop in 1838], those who have thus been tithed shall pay one-tenth of all their interest annually; and this shall be a standing law unto them forever, for my holy priesthood, saith the Lord' [D&C 119:4].

"For many years, presidents of the Church have interpreted 'interest'as 'income.' Beyond that, they have not elaborated. That fourth verse consists of thirty-five words. Contrast that with the cumbersome and complex tax codes enacted and enforced by governments."[44]

Those thirty-five words have made a profound difference in the lives of many people. You've probably sat in Church meetings and heard stories from people who have experienced miraculous blessings because they followed this command to pay one-tenth of their interest annually. Our family does not have a miraculous story to share from our personal experience, but I will say this—there have been years when we have struggled financially. I can remember months when our medical bills took every extra dollar we had, and we had to scrape by to pay for the heat and the water and the phones. And yet, our needs were always met. Always. Our kids knew what it was to grow up counting pennies, but they also knew ours was a family that paid tithing. Always.

The Lord took care of the rest.

It is so simple. So straightforward. That one verse contains a principle that leads to great promise. —EBF

Reflect and Respond
What blessings have you experienced from paying your tithing?

Your favorite
scripture in
Section 119

DOCTRINE AND COVENANTS 120:1

And by mine own voice . . .

In the last week of the Lord's life, He spent a few days teaching in the temple court-yards in Jerusalem. On one of those days, He took a minute to point out to His disciples a poor widow bringing her tithing funds into the temple treasury. She dropped in just two mites, coins worth less than a penny in today's currency. In the hustle and bustle of a temple crowded during a Jewish festival, it would be reasonable to think that the woman could easily have gone unnoticed—but not by the Lord. He saw her, and He saw her humble offering.

After the Lord reaffirmed the law of consecration and gave a new system of practicing it in the latter days, He organized in this revelation the council of people who would oversee and have stewardship for all the funds collected. The group included the First Presidency, the Quorum of the Twelve, and the Presiding Bishopric. This same group makes up the council today for the use of tithing funds. In addition to those mentioned, the Lord also says His own voice will be involved in the decisions for the tithing money. That is still true today as well. President Gordon B. Hinckley, a modern disciple who sat on that council for many years, once said: "I keep on the credenza behind my desk a widow's mite that was given me in Jerusalem many years ago as a reminder, a constant reminder, of the sanctity of the funds with which we have to deal. They come from the widow, they are her offering . . . and they are to be used with care and discretion for the purposes of the Lord."[45] It seems as if the Lord still notices the widow and is still pointing her out to His disciples. —DB

Reflect and Respond

How does it make you feel to know that the Lord knows your offering and is personally involved in using it to fulfill His purposes?

Your favorite scripture in Section 120

DOCTRINE AND COVENANTS 121:1

O God, where art thou?

Joseph's hand must have been shaking with cold while he wrote this line in a letter to the Saints from a dungeon prison in Liberty, Missouri. He and several other men had been wrongfully accused and thrown into a basement cell with awful conditions for some of the coldest months of the year. Yet, as I read the letter, I feel that his concerns were not so much for his own welfare as for that of his fellow Saints, who were being beaten, plundered, and driven from their homes.

Normally, jail cells are reserved for and filled with the guilty. During these months, they were occupied by the innocent—an innocent servant of God who spent the days and nights pleading for His help. Every time I read the first few words of this section, my heart aches. "O God, where art thou?" Perhaps those who received the letter were wondering the same thing. Where was He? Why was He not intervening?

These are questions that are asked by millions around the world as they suffer injustice and wrong despite their efforts to do good. Some might wonder if God is unable to help them. Joseph wrote as a part of his prayers, "O Lord God Almighty, maker of heaven, earth, and seas, and of all things that in them are, and who controllest and subjectest the devil, . . . stretch forth thy hand" (D&C 121:4). These are words that seem to say, "I know You can help! I know You have the power! So why aren't You helping?"

The letter includes not only Joseph's prayer but also the Lord's answer. "Peace be unto thy soul; thine adversity and thine afflictions shall be but a small moment" (D&C 121:7). We don't know why He allows what He allows and why He intervenes when He intervenes, but we do know that He cares. The revelation is evidence of that. —DB

Reflect and Respond

When have you known that God was there even if He didn't change your circumstances? What does it mean to you to know He is there?

Your favorite scripture in Section 121

DOCTRINE AND COVENANTS 122:1–2

The ends of the earth shall inquire after thy name, and fools shall have thee in derision . . . while the pure in heart, and the wise . . . shall seek counsel, and authority, and blessings constantly from under thy hand.

When Joseph was seventeen years old, living in an obscure farm town in upstate New York, an angel came to his bedroom in the middle of the night and prophesied to him that his name "should be had for good and evil among all nations, kindreds, and tongues, or that it should be both good and evil spoken of among all people" (Joseph Smith—History 1:33). How many languages do you think he knew? How many countries had he been to? Do you think he doubted such a bold and startling statement? Almost sixteen years later, and a thousand miles away, Joseph was sitting in a dungeon prison when the Lord said something similar to him. Would it be true? Would people all over the earth inquire about him? Would people seek his counsel and blessings? He was in jail—it must have seemed like rock bottom. And yet both prophecies have been fulfilled in a way Joseph might not have even imagined.

I once asked some institute students to indicate by show of hands whether any of them had heard Joseph's name and mission mocked. Most people raised their hands. I then asked if any of them had heard of people inquiring after him and seeking after blessings from the mission he was called to. Most people raised their hands again. But the next question was even better. "What place and language did it happen in?" The answers were enlightening: Korea. Brazil. St. George. Alabama. Iceland. Next door. I then asked which of them had had the privilege of fulfilling the prophecy themselves. Testimonies of the goodness of God came pouring in. Moroni was right when he spoke the prophecy in his bedroom, and the Lord was right in Liberty Jail. All over the world, fools still mock, but the wise are seeking for the blessings that the Lord poured out onto the earth through Joseph. —DB

Reflect and Respond

What blessings, counsel, and authority have been a benefit to you from the mission of the Prophet Joseph Smith?

Your favorite scripture in Section 122

DOCTRINE AND COVENANTS 123:17

Therefore, dearly beloved brethren, **let us cheerfully do all things that lie in our power;** and then may we stand still, with the utmost assurance, to see the salvation of God, and for his arm to be revealed.

I once overheard my son's basketball coach trying to encourage and pump up his team in the remaining thirty-two seconds of their game. They were down by a substantial amount of points, they were outmatched, and they were out of time. I appreciated his enthusiasm, but everyone in the room knew there was no chance of their winning.

Life can look like that sometimes.

It did for Joseph—several times. But on this particular occasion, still sitting on the straw and stone of the Liberty Jail floor, with no prospects of being set free, Joseph wrote to the Saints—who were living in makeshift structures on borrowed land with no money, and no hope—to cheerfully do all that they could, and to wait and watch for the Lord to do His greatest work.

Maybe some who read the letter felt like I did listening to the basketball coach. Perhaps some wondered—at what point do we just give up? What good does it do anymore? No, my son's game did not end in a miraculous victory, but Joseph's story—which was really God's story—has. The prisoners were eventually released, a beautiful temple was built, and the ripple effects of the Restoration are currently flooding the earth. Joseph wasn't living all of that at the time, but he did sense it. He was confident in it because He was confident in God. His advice is still golden today. Writing from a jail cell, Joseph counseled his friends to be cheerful, move forward, and then sit still with assurance that God will always win. This advice got the Saints through the martyrdom, through the trek, and it is still inspiring those who are down and out in the fourth quarter today. —DB

Reflect and Respond

What is the difference between doing everything in your power and "cheerfully" doing all things in your power?

Your favorite scripture in **Section 123**

DOCTRINE AND COVENANTS 124:100

. . . and what if . . .

From her kitchen window in Nauvoo, Sarah Granger Kimball watched the Nauvoo Temple being built. The Lord said of the temple site, "If ye labor with all your might, I will consecrate that spot that it shall be made holy" (D&C 124:44). Sarah wanted to labor with all her might to help with the building process. Take a minute to consider that phrase, *if you labor with all your might.*

Because of Sarah's wish to help with the temple, the idea for the Relief Society was born. That is the miracle that can come from entering into a "what if" with the Lord.

On the other hand, consider William Law. He also lived in Nauvoo at the time the temple was being built. In this section, the Lord counseled him to be humble and without guile, to mount up in the imagination of his thoughts as if on eagle's wings. "And what if . . ." the Lord said to William Law, *what if I would that you should raise the dead? Don't withhold your voice* (see D&C 124:100). *What if . . .*

It was as if nothing could hold William back from the great things the Lord held in store for him. But William Law did not follow the counsel of the Lord. In April 1844, William Law, who had served in the First Presidency, was excommunicated. Instead of those great things, William published an anti-Mormon paper. It was the printing and destruction of that newspaper and printing press that actually led to the arrest and martyrdom of Joseph Smith.

Isn't it amazing how those two simple words—*what if*—can go two completely different ways? The building up of a society. The death of a prophet. I think of these two stories and wonder about the "what if" the Lord has in store for me. —EBF

Reflect and Respond

Is there anything you are doing that might limit the Lord's ability to perform great things in your life?

Your favorite scripture in **Section 124**

DOCTRINE AND COVENANTS 125:2

Let them gather themselves together . . .
and build up cities unto my name.

The first decade of our married life was hard. We struggled through difficult pregnancies, financial stress, and all the challenges newly married couples have. One afternoon I was pondering our life and realized the journey of each of my children so far had been a source of teaching very important lessons. Caleb had taught me wisdom. Josh had taught me courage and strength. I remember waiting for Meg to come and praying every night that we would have a season of joy with her. For Megan's birth, I invited all the women in my family to be there in the room. It was a celebration. My first daughter was welcomed into the world by the women who would surround her as she grew. It was a special moment of joy that Greg and I will never forget. Ten months later, Josh would be diagnosed with juvenile diabetes at the age of three. But for that short season, our little home was overflowing with joy.

When I read section 125 after coming off of the chapters on trial and affliction, it reminds me of an important truth. In life there are Nauvoo moments and Liberty Jail moments—moments of peace and moments of discouragement. Nauvoo was filled with evenings when couples would wander the streets and knock on the door of any home that had a candle burning in the window as a welcome. Those came right on the heels of the Liberty Jail nights of sleeping on cold, hard rock floors.

I have learned sweet lessons from that jail cell and from walking the streets of Nauvoo. What I know of a surety is that the Lord will meet us in both places. He plans to celebrate those moments of joy and to weep through the days of sorrow.

He meets us where we are. —EBF

Reflect and Respond

Are you in a Liberty Jail moment or a Nauvoo moment? What are you learning there?

Your favorite
scripture in
Section 125

DOCTRINE AND COVENANTS 126:1-2

Dear and **well-beloved brother, Brigham** . . . I have seen
your labor and toil in journeyings for my name.

A few years ago, I had a conversation with someone who was unfamiliar with Brigham Young, and when his name was brought up, he asked, in sincerity, "Isn't he the man who had so many wives?" I felt awful that of all Brigham did to shoulder the burden of the ongoing Restoration, that was all that person knew about him. It felt to me like someone asking if Abraham Lincoln was that guy who wore a tall hat. I wanted to tell him about Brigham's faithful heart and his loyalty to the Lord. I wanted him to know how Brigham left almost immediately after joining the Church with his brother to preach the gospel of Christ on his first mission. That when he went with Zion's Camp to help rescue and redeem his brothers and sisters, he and his brother were known as the "sweet wingers" because of how joyful they were on such a miserable trip. Or about his missions to the Eastern States—to New York, Vermont, Massachusetts, and Rhode Island. Or the mission to England, where, in his words, "Through the mercy of God we have gained many friends, established churches in almost every noted town and city in the Kingdom of Great Britain, baptized between seven and eight thousand souls, printed 5000 Books of Mormon, 3000 Hymn Books, 2500 volumes of the Millennial Star, and 50,000 tracts."[46]

When Brigham returned from that mission, he found his family destitute, in a single-room cabin, in pitiful conditions, and he went right to work to make life better for them. It was then that the Lord called him well-beloved and let him know He had watched every step of his faithful footsteps.

I'm certain He has seen the same and feels the same of you. —DB

Reflect and Respond

Describe a moment when you have felt the shine of the Lord's approval on the sacred toilings you have been through.

Your favorite
scripture in
Section 126

DOCTRINE AND COVENANTS 127:2

Deep water is what I am wont to swim in.

Joseph began this section by writing about pretensions "founded in falsehood of the blackest dye" (D&C 127:1). I know that dye: the kind that won't ever come off, the stain that seems permanent. Then Joseph moves to the storm: the one that hasn't blown over, the peril through which he has been called to pass. "Deep water is what I am wont to swim in" (D&C 127:2), Joseph writes to the Saints in Nauvoo and describes how the envy and wrath of men have followed him all the days of his life. How he has learned to glory in persecution. How the Lord continues to deliver him.

"God knoweth all these things, whether it be good or bad" (D&C 127:2), Joseph reminds the Saints, and I take great comfort from his wisdom. *God knoweth all these things.* He knows everything. The good and the bad. The black stain. The storm that won't blow over. The peril. The deep water. *He knows.* That verse gives me so much strength.

Because if He knows about the storm, He knows about the rainbow. And the stain remover. And the still water. And sometimes getting through the hard stuff is easier when you are walking the broken road with someone who *knows*.

I remember once asking a crowd of people to raise their hands if there was a moment in their lives that only God knew about. Every single hand was raised. I found comfort in that. There are things that are between just you and God, the One who knows all things—including the season you are in now and the season that is coming next.

If you are swimming in deep water or waiting for the storm to blow over, please remember you are not alone. *God knoweth all these things* (D&C 127:2), and He will not leave you to weather this storm alone. —EBF

....

Reflect and Respond
How have you come to trust that God knoweth all things? How has that verse gotten you through a hard time in your life?

Your favorite scripture in Section 127

DOCTRINE AND COVENANTS 128:19

Now, what do we hear in
the gospel which we have received?

This is such a good question to ponder. What do we hear in this gospel? Perhaps your answer would be negative—there are too many commandments, it's too strict, the culture is filled with perfectionism. That wasn't Joseph's answer. Five times he tells us what the gospel means to him, and five times he uses the same word: *gladness*.

I love that word.

It comes to mind as I think of the people we have met: Joseph Knight, who was a friend to Joseph; Emma, who was there even in the seventh trouble; Oliver Cowdery, who at the end of his life just wanted to be identified with the Church; David Whitmer, who was called to assist; Martin Harris, who went from wicked man to witness. Oliver Granger, who learned that sacrifice is more important than increase, and his daughter, Sarah Granger Kimball, whose kitchen-window thoughts led to the building up of an entire women's organization. Jane James, who walked eight hundred miles on foot to meet the Prophet. Captain Fearnot, who counseled, "Whatever you do, do not deny the faith." And a young, obscure boy of no consequence in the world, who learned for himself about the gospel of Jesus Christ. I think of glad tidings from Cumorah, angels from heaven, miracles on the banks of the Susquehanna, the keys of the kingdom.

It was the memory of all these places and people that confirmed Joseph's hope and caused him to proclaim, "Courage, brethren; and on, on to the victory! Let your hearts rejoice, and be exceedingly glad" (D&C 128:22).

It makes me wonder, where does my gladness in this gospel come from? What would my list of glad tidings look like? What do we hear in this gospel? —EBF

Reflect and Respond

List some of the people, places, and promises you have learned about in the Doctrine and Covenants. Which bring you the most gladness?

Your favorite
scripture in
Section 128

DOCTRINE AND COVENANTS 129:9

. . . three grand keys . . .

Many years ago, I was in a stake conference when a man stood up and talked about a dream he had had several nights before. In the dream there were three keys, and the keys fit into three locks on his front door that would keep his family safe.

For many days afterward, he thought about those keys. What were they? What would keep his family safe? After spending time in prayer, he received the answer—family prayer, family scripture study, and family home evening. He went out and bought three keys to hang in his home as a reminder.

I did the same thing. I loved the thought of spiritually protecting my family with three keys.

When I read this section in the Doctrine and Covenants, that story came immediately to mind. I couldn't help but think of another Father who was worried about protecting His earthly family. He spoke of "three grand keys" that would help each of us know if an administration was from God. Those three keys are found in this short section and help us to identify whether messengers from beyond the veil have been sent from God.

This section helps me view our Father in Heaven as a protector. He is a Father who will send messengers to help us along the way, and who wants to make sure we recognize those messengers. He is a Father who wants to keep each of His families safe. —EBF

Reflect and Respond

As you read through this section, see if you can discover the three grand keys. How will they help to protect you?

Your favorite
scripture in
Section 129

DOCTRINE AND COVENANTS 130:18

Whatever principle of intelligence we attain unto
in this life, it will rise with us in the resurrection.

Today, sitting down with the prophet would be quite a difficult thing to arrange. A simple handshake or a selfie would be a once-in-a-lifetime opportunity for most. I once got a chance to shake the prophet's hand. It took some snaking and squeezing through a crowd to get there, but I made it. It is a cherished memory for me, but there was not much to it. He doesn't remember it, I'm sure—all we did was exchange quick hellos, and I offered a simple, sincere thank you from Jenny and me. Odds are it will not happen again.

But things were a little different in the Nauvoo days. Joseph was busy, but a person's odds of getting a one-on-one with him were much higher. I wonder what kind of conversation you would have chosen to have with him if you got the opportunity. One of those interactions is recorded in the Doctrine and Covenants as section 130. It was actually a dinner conversation between Joseph and others at his sister's house.[47] William Clayton, Joseph's secretary, wrote down the answers to some of the questions they were asking, questions about the nature of God, the Second Coming, the Millennium, and more. Some of the questions were from Joseph. Wouldn't you want to sit in on that question-and-answer session? I love thinking about this little group gathered together, wondering and seeking and yearning to learn more about who God is and how they could attain His attributes. I love that some of their questions brought answers and some of them brought more questions. But whatever they gained from the gathering—both together as people and also the gathering of knowledge and experience—they took it with them. It left an imprint on their soul. —DB

Reflect and Respond

What impact has gathering and questioning and studying had on your soul?

Your favorite scripture in
Section 130

DOCTRINE AND COVENANTS 131:4

He cannot have an increase . . .

I love planting a garden. I live for it. At the end of March, I start counting down the number of days to the weekend after Mother's Day (which is the best weekend to plant if you live in Utah). I love the feel of freshly tilled soil running through my hands, the smell of the earth in spring, the water running down the trenches as we prepare the ground for growth. I am good at planting.

I'm not as good at growing things. I have ruined zucchini and spaghetti squash by planting them too close together. My broccoli plants got destroyed by bugs. I always end up with way too many tomato plants because that is the one kind of plant I never kill. I also love trying new things, like artichokes or cantaloupe. It doesn't deter me that I am bad at the growing, I still try again every year.

I think that's why I fell in love with the scripture in First Corinthians about gardening: "I have planted, Apollos watered; but God gave the increase. So then neither is he that planteth any thing, neither he that watereth; but God that giveth the increase" (1 Corinthians 3:6–7). We can plant, and we can water, but God gives the increase. He knows the growing season. He has planned out the harvest. He will be in charge of the increase.

My study has led me to realize that increase is one of the most important parts of God's plan for His children. It is one of His greatest gifts. In the end, mortality is about progression and increase and potential. God is doing what He does best: growing things. In section 131 we are reminded about the highest degree, the place of greatest increase. God's gift—a kingdom of harvesting and gathering and reaping.

A place of increase with an offering of abundance. —EBF

Reflect and Respond

Ponder the principle of increase. Where do you see it in scripture? What do you learn from your studies?

Your favorite scripture in Section 131

DOCTRINE AND COVENANTS 132:24

This is eternal lives—**to know the only wise and true God,
and Jesus Christ,** whom he hath sent. I am he.

Hyrum Smith, the faithful brother of the Prophet, returned to Joseph after trying to give Emma a copy of the revelation that included some of the principles of plural marriage, and said he had never received a more severe lecture in his life. According to William Clayton, Joseph's secretary, who was there, Joseph quietly remarked, "I told you, you did not know Emma as well as I did."[48] Joseph then put the revelation in his pocket, and they both left the office.

Even now, more than 175 years later, I can almost sense the heaviness in the room and in Joseph's heart. Volumes have been written on the topic, and they are important to read and understand, but as I read the revelation, I think about the people and the relationships involved. I think of Joseph torn between the commandments of the Lord and the unimaginably sensitive situation with Emma. I think of her struggle to understand, support, rely, and receive. I think of Hyrum and others who strained spiritually to accept the will of the Lord given through an imperfect prophet they knew better than anyone. Hyrum said, after his own personal battle to come to understand, "The doctrine is so plain, I can convince any reasonable man or woman of its truth, purity and heavenly origin."[49]

The doctrine might eventually become plain, but the situations it created were complicated. It seems like all relationship are. But cradled in the revelation is a truth about relationships that is at the heart and center of not just this issue but our life on earth—to come to know the Father and the Son. That is eternal life. And it is often through struggles that that particular relationship becomes solidified. —DB

Reflect and Respond
What difficult situations or faith struggles have led you to know God more?

Your favorite
scripture in
Section 132

DOCTRINE AND COVENANTS 133:2

The Lord who shall suddenly come . . .

It had been a hard weekend. My dear friend was trying to negotiate her fourth battle with cancer. The emotion of it all was wearing us thin. I can remember showing up to teach seminary that day and walking into the early-morning prayer meeting, which was how we started every day. "You look exhausted," the principal said as I walked through the door. "I am," I told him, "I'm done with mortality." It was a bold statement, and I must have looked really serious when I said it, because the principal went into help mode. "What's going on?" and "How can I help?" were the next two phrases out of his mouth. "Oh, I'm okay," I told him, "I'm just done with this mortality thing. Let's call it. Let's end it." He raised his eyebrows, with a look of concern on his face, and I continued, "After weekends like this, I just have two words—Send Jesus."

Weekends like that are the reason I love sections like Doctrine and Covenants 133. Some people are afraid of these Second Coming chapters. I can understand that, but for some reason they inspire me with hope of good things to come. Some of the verses talk of terrible things, but others speak of great promises: "For since the beginning of the world have not men heard nor perceived by the ear, neither hath any eye seen, O God, besides thee, how great things thou hast prepared for him that waiteth for thee" (D&C 133:45).

I'm ready for the great things, especially when mortality feels exhausting.

You might be interested to know that I made T-shirts that week for me and my friend to wear on the hardest days. They have just two words written on the front, bold white letters stark against the red shirt: *Send Jesus.*

One of these days, He will. —EBF

Reflect and Respond

What are your favorite Second Coming promises? As you read through D&C 133, write some of those great things down.

Your favorite scripture in Section 133

DOCTRINE AND COVENANTS 134:1

We believe that governments were instituted of God for the benefit of man; and that **he holds men accountable** for their acts in relation to them, . . . for the good and safety of society.

Recently, a whistleblower made accusations against The Church of Jesus Christ of Latter-day Saints for its accounting practices and use of tithing and offering funds. This is not the first time or the last time that the Church will encounter questions and concerns in regard to its relationship to the governments in the countries it is established in. And people should certainly ask such questions. The Church was established to preach the gospel and offer the new and everlasting covenant to all the people of the world, but Church members commit to do this according to principles intended to help us carefully honor both the laws and the cultures of the different people we work among. This requires the work and expertise of people of every kind. That was the pattern established in the beginning days of the Church, and it was written as an official statement and document to be printed in the first issue of the Doctrine and Covenants. It includes principles the Church still refers to as it navigates new issues and circumstances every year.

When my wife, Jenny, went to Jerusalem to study at the BYU Jerusalem Center, she had to sign papers and make promises that she would not share the gospel of Jesus Christ while there as a student. This went against what she felt compelled to do, but she also knew that maintaining a good and safe society included obeying the rules. It also seems as if our maintaining a relationship with fellow brothers and sisters is more important to the Lord than pushing a cause. Or perhaps that actually is our cause—to become one with those brothers and sisters. —DB

Reflect and Respond

What are some principles you live by to be anxiously engaged in sharing the gospel while also maintaining good relationships?

Your favorite scripture in Section 134

DOCTRINE AND COVENANTS 135:3

Joseph Smith, the Prophet and Seer of the Lord, has
done more, **save Jesus only,** for the salvation of men in
this world, than any other man that ever lived in it.

John Taylor became a dear friend to Joseph—so much so that he went with him into Carthage Jail when he himself had not been arrested, compelled, or asked to go. He was there in the room on the fateful day when Joseph and Hyrum, his heroes and companions, were martyred. It happened in front of his eyes.

John wrote a document as one of the witnesses of the martyrdom and included this bold claim about his prophet friend. Every time it is read out loud, I imagine that Joseph squirms a little. I think the same thing every time we sing "Praise to the man who communed with Jehovah." I can almost hear Joseph saying, "Oh, thank you, but can we please sing 'Praise to Jehovah who communed with the man?'"

It was the Lord who called him. It was the Lord who gave him strength to endure. It is His truth and goodness that sustains the Church today. Perhaps when we count it all up, yes, we have learned more about Jesus through the ministry of Joseph Smith than through anyone else, and that makes John Taylor right.

We know above all that Jesus is the only Savior—that is what Joseph taught us. But, much as we cannot help but have tender feelings for our mom or teacher or friend who taught us about our Savior, we cannot help wanting to honor and thank and love Joseph for all he sacrificed to bring that knowledge of Him to us. I just can't help it. I'm a lover of Jesus, but when I cross into the spirit world, I am going to take my kids to meet Joseph. And when we meet him, and I thank him, I imagine he will say: "Oh, don't fuss over me. Can I introduce you to Him?" And I will say back, "Oh, my friend, you already have." —DB

Reflect and Respond

How has Joseph Smith's ministry and all that was revealed through him helped you come closer to Jesus Christ?

Your favorite
scripture in
Section 135

DOCTRINE AND COVENANTS 136:28

If thou art merry, praise the Lord with singing, with music,
with dancing, and with a prayer of praise and thanksgiving.

Latter-day Saint midwife Patty Sessions wrote in her journal: "About six o'clock in the morning I was called for to go back two miles. It then snowed. . . . I found the sister that I was called to see in an old log cabin. Her child was born before I got there. She rode thirteen miles after she was in travail, and crossed the creek on a log after dark."[50] That was a little bit of the story of one of the babies that Patty, who traveled with the first company across the plains to the Salt Lake Valley, helped to deliver and take care of. She is known to have delivered at least nine babies on the banks of the Mississippi River, and several more during the journey.

When Brigham was in Winter Quarters, a temporary city on the border of Nebraska and Iowa, he received this particular revelation on how to organize and counsel the Saints as they made their trip to their new home. They were organized into companies to help each other across—companies of people like Patty and the woman who crossed the creek on a log as she was in labor.

There are so many stories of individuals who grew and learned and changed as they participated in this part of their journey. A snapshot of the trek might as well be a snapshot of humanity—each person living, growing, and learning in his or her own journey. The advice to praise and dance and give thanks seems appropriate, even on snowy days. It was advice Brigham gave and took. According to Patty, one day she saw "Brother Brigham came up with his company driving his teams in the rain and mud to his knees, as happy as a king." —DB

Reflect and Respond

How have laughter, praise, and thanksgiving given you strength in your journey?

Your favorite
scripture in
Section 136

DOCTRINE AND COVENANTS 137:5-6

I saw Father Adam and Abraham; and my father and my mother;
my brother Alvin, that has long since slept; **and marveled . . .**

When Joseph saw a vision of the celestial kingdom, he saw streets paved with gold, a flaming gate at the entrance, and the throne of God. He also saw Abraham, the ancient prophet, and Adam, the father of all mankind.

He saw his mother and father (who were both still alive) in the kingdom as well. But the person who caused him to "marvel" when he saw him, the one person who might have taken his breath away, was his older brother Alvin.

For thirteen years, Joseph and his family had carried the burden and sadness of the death of their kind, gentle Alvin. When he died tragically, Joseph was just eighteen years old. He said, "I remember well the pangs of sorrow that swelled my youthful bosom and almost burst my tender heart when he died."[51]

Alvin was Joseph's hero. He was a hard worker, a fierce defender of Joseph, and seemed to be the family member most excited about the Book of Mormon plates. Alvin died before Joseph ever received them, and his dying wish for Joseph was to do everything he could—to be a good boy—so he could receive them. William, Joseph's younger brother, remembered at the funeral the pastor implying "very strongly that he had gone to hell, for Alvin was not a church member, but he was a good boy, and my father did not like it."[52] The Smiths struggled with the contradiction of the goodness of a loving God and the words of that religious leader for over a decade. Then, one night in the Kirtland Temple, Joseph learned the beautiful truth—a truth that made him and the whole world marvel. God was merciful. God was love. Alvin was safe. —DB

Reflect and Respond

What truths have thrilled your heart, brought you peace, or caused you to marvel?

Your favorite scripture in Section 137

DOCTRINE AND COVENANTS 138:16

They were assembled **awaiting the advent of the
Son of God** . . . to declare their redemption.

The year 1918 was plagued with tragedy. World War I, which would ultimately claim twenty million lives, was cursing the world. A worldwide flu pandemic had killed fifty million people, with more than 195,000 Americans dying during the month of October 1918 alone. That was the month when Joseph F. Smith saw his vision of the spirit world. Earlier that year, in January, he had lost his own oldest son to a sudden medical emergency. This was after a life dotted with tragedy: he lost his father and mother early and buried a wife and eleven children.[53]

His heart ached for the world, for the Church he led, and for his own family. It is no wonder he pondered and thought deeply about the state of those who had passed on. More specifically, Joseph F. Smith wrote that it was while he was "reflecting upon the great atoning sacrifice that was made by the Son of God" that this vision was opened to him (D&C 138:2).

For the first time in this dispensation, and perhaps ever, the Lord revealed a glorious vision of how good He was to those who had left us—tragically or otherwise. In the vision, Joseph F. Smith saw those who were gathered together, waiting for their redemption. Sometimes I wonder if he felt particularly tender about those verses, for they described the state of the hearts of so many who deal with tragedy—waiting for redemption. Waiting for their miracles. Waiting for the coming of the Son of God. That is a day that will come for all of us, but in a beautiful way, the giving of this vision was a way that He was showing us that He is already here. The impact and power of His great sacrifice are already at work, and the benefits and sweetness of it can be opened to us even now. —DB

Reflect and Respond

What has waiting on the Lord been like for you?

Your favorite
scripture in
Section 138

OFFICIAL DECLARATION 1

This is the question I lay before the Latter-day Saints. You have to judge for yourselves. . . . I leave this with you, for you to contemplate and consider. **The Lord is at work with us.**

In 1890, Wilford Woodruff presented a declaration to the Church and world that the Church was not practicing and would not practice plural marriage anymore in the United States. According to President Woodruff, the decision was made by revelation. This causes people to wonder: Why was there a revelation to begin plural marriage if there was going to be one to end it? And why did the revelation come *after* people were imprisoned and the Church's property and temples were being threatened with takeover?

Was it revelation or just reaction?

President Woodruff reminded the Saints that he was willing to allow all of the Church's property to be surrendered and all of its leaders to face trial and imprisonment if God commanded him to continue the practice. Like Joseph Smith, he was willing to pay the price of obedience to the Lord. As you read his words, you can hear the struggle and the wonder in his tone. The decision was messy. It seems as if God allows prophets to contemplate and consider and wrestle with issues the same way He allows us to.

When you read the declaration, you can see evidence of this wrestle, of the contemplating and considering. The invitation from the prophet to the Church members was for them to do the same. And that is thrilling. He leaves it to us and invites us on the same journey. The question is: Is the Lord in it or not? Is it His work or isn't it? As we consider and contemplate, we can come to find the answer for ourselves. We are invited to receive an answer directly from the Lord—on this issue or any other. —DB

Reflect and Respond

What do you think it looks like to contemplate and consider? Why is this so important in the revelation process?

Your favorite passage in Official Declaration 1

OFFICIAL DECLARATION 2

Aware of the promises made . . . and witnessing the faithfulness of those from whom the priesthood has been withheld, we have pleaded long and earnestly . . . and by revelation [the Lord] has confirmed that the long-promised day has come.

Jenny was insistent on naming our first little girl Jane. I was against it—until I learned the story of Jane Manning James, one of the first and most faithful black converts.

I learned of her leading a group of her family members to Nauvoo, walking eight hundred miles barefoot, leaving bloody prints in the snow, and sleeping often out in the open winter air. She had been denied passage on a ship because of the color of her skin, but that wasn't going to stop her from doing what it took to gather with the Saints.

Her faith in God and love of the gospel propelled her forward her whole life—through persecution, death of children, divorce, her trek west, and desperate poverty. Perhaps more painful than all of these was being denied her temple blessings, just like passage on that ship, because of her race. Even after her continual petitions to the leaders of the Church, and despite her faith, love, and devotion to the gospel of Jesus Christ and her endearing friendship with Joseph and Emma, the answer always came back as no. And still Jane kept the faith. She even donated to the building of temples she would never get to enter.

There is no record as to why a ban on the priesthood blessings came in the history of the Church. But there is a record as to why the blessings returned. It was the faith of people like Jane Manning James that led to the petitions and eventual answered prayers and promises from God that all His children could "receive every blessing of the gospel." That's the kind of faith I hope my daughter Jane inherits. —DB

Reflect and Respond

When has the faith of someone else inspired your own faith?

Your favorite passage in Official Declaration 2

NOTES

1. *Teachings of the Prophet Joseph Smith* (1976), 361.
2. See "Letter from Elder W. H. Kelly," *Saints' Herald*, March 1, 1882, 67.
3. See *The Joseph Smith Papers, Documents: Volume 1, July 1828–June 1831* (2013), 13–22.
4. *Joseph Smith Papers, Documents: Volume 1*, 47–48.
5. Steven C. Harper, *Making Sense of the Doctrine and Covenants* (2008), 54.
6. Boyd K. Packer, "The Shield of Faith," *Ensign*, May 1995.
7. N. Eldon Tanner, "Put on the Whole Armor of God," *Ensign*, May 1979.
8. Parley P. Pratt, *The Autobiography of Parley P. Pratt,* ed. Parley P. Pratt Jr. (1938), 27.
9. See *Joseph Smith Papers, Documents: Volume 1*, 206.
10. https://www.josephsmithpapers.org/paper-summary/revelation-4-november-1830-dc-34/1#source-note (Page 45).
11. Newel Knight, "Autobiography and Journal, 1846," Church History Library, Salt Lake City.
12. "John Whitmer, History, 1831–circa 1847," 26, josephsmithpapers.org.
13. Ezra Taft Benson, "Listen to a Prophet's Voice," *Ensign*, January 1973.
14. https://www.josephsmithpapers.org/paper-summary/letter-to-william-w-phelps-22-july-1840/2.
15. "A Bishop unto the Church," *Revelations in Context,* history.lds.org
16. https://www.josephsmithpapers.org/paper-summary/revelation-11-september-1831-dc-64/1 (Page 108).
17. Matthew C. Godfrey, "William McLellin's Five Questions," in *Revelations in Context,* history.lds.org.
18. https://www.josephsmithpapers.org/paper-summary/revelation-1-november-1831-a-dc-68/1 (Page 113).
19. Harper, *Making Sense of the Doctrine and Covenants,* page ?
20. https://www.josephsmithpapers.org/paper-summary/vision-16-february-1832-dc-76/1 (Page 1).
21. *Teachings of the Prophet Joseph Smith* (1976), 11.
22. *The Joseph Smith Papers, Documents: Volume 2, July 1831–January 1833* (2013), 209.
23. https://www.josephsmithpapers.org/paper-summary/revelation-26-april-1832-dc-82/1 (Page 128).
24. Harper, *Making Sense of the Doctrine and Covenants*, 294.
25. *Joseph Smith Papers, Documents: Volume 2*, 316.
26. "Minutes of the General Conference," Tuesday, Sept. 9, 1851, afternoon session, in *Millennial Star*, vol. 14 (February 1, 1852), 35.
27. See Brent M. Rogers, "Vienna Jaques: Woman of Faith," *Ensign,* June 2016.
28. Nancy Clement Williams, *After 100 Years* (1951), 77.
29. Joseph Fielding McConkie and Craig J. Ostler, *Revelations of the Restoration* (2000), 699–700.
30. *The Joseph Smith Papers, Documents: Volume 3, February 1833–March 1834* (2014), 221–28.

31. *Joseph Smith Papers, Documents: Volume 3*, 320–25.

32. *Autobiography of Parley P. Pratt*, 102.

33. https://www.josephsmithpapers.org/paper-summary/minute-book-1/31 (Page 27).

34. https://www.churchofjesuschrist.org/manual/doctrine-and-covenants-student-manual/section-105-revelation-to-zions-camp.

35. Delbert L. Stapley, in https://www.churchofjesuschrist.org/manual/doctrine-and-covenants-student-manual/section-105-revelation-to-zions-camp.

36. Leonard J. Arrington, "The John Tanner Family," *Ensign*, March 1979.

37. *The Joseph Smith Papers, Documents: Volume 4, April 1834–September 1835* (2016), 180–82.

38. *The Joseph Smith Papers, Documents: Volume 5, October 1834–January 1838* (2017), 122–23.

39. Thomas B. Marsh, in *Journal of Discourses,* 26 vols. (1854–1886), 5:206–7.

40. https://www.josephsmithpapers.org/paper-summary/history-1838-1856-volume-c-1-2-november-1838-31-july-1842/194 (Page 1022).

41. Lycurgus A. Wilson, *Life of David W. Patten: The First Apostolic Martyr* [1904], 16; Susan Easton Black, *Who's Who in the Doctrine and Covenants*, [1997] 218.

42. Russell M. Nelson, "The Correct Name of the Church," *Ensign*, November 2018.

43. Wilford Woodruff, in *Journal of Discourses,* 13:159.

44. Gordon B. Hinckley, "The Sacred Law of Tithing," *Ensign*, December 1989.

45. Gordon B. Hinckley, "This Thing Was Not Done in a Corner," Ensign, November 1996.

46. McConkie and Ostler, *Revelations of the Restoration*, 990.

47. https://www.josephsmithpapers.org/paper-summary/instruction-2-april-1843-as-reported-by-william-clayton/1.

48. *History of The Church of Jesus Christ of Latter-Day Saints*, 6 vols. (1932–1951), 5:32–33.

49. *History of the Church*, 5:32.

50. Claire Noall, "Mormon Midwives," *Utah Historical Quarterly*, vol. 10 (1942): 87–88.

51. "The Book of the Law of the Lord," August 23, 1842, cited in *History of the Church*, 5:126–27.

52. J. S. Peterson interview with William Smith, 1893, *Zion's Ensign,* January 13, 1894; this section was reprinted in *Latter-day Saints' Millennial Star,* February 26, 1894, 133.

53. Harper, *Making Sense of the Doctrine and Covenants*, 508–9.

ABOUT THE AUTHORS

EMILY BELLE FREEMAN is a best-selling author and popular inspirational speaker. She has a deep love of the scriptures, which comes from a desire to find their application in everyday life. She is the author of numerous books, including *Grace Where You Are*; *Creating a Christ-Centered Home*; *Closer to Christ*; and *Even This: Getting to the Place Where You Can Trust God with Anything*. She is a favorite speaker at Time Out for Women and a cohost with David Butler of *Don't Miss This*, a *Come, Follow Me* study channel on YouTube. Her greatest joy comes from spending time with her family. Read more at emilybellefreeman.com and follow Emily on Instagram and Facebook @emilybellefreeman.

DAVID BUTLER'S greatest love is people. He has adopted as a life motto: "Stuff no mattah, people mattah." His favorite people are his wife, Jenny, and their six darling children. Some of his other loves include good food, spontaneous adventures, Christmas morning, and the sea. David cohosts the popular YouTube scripture study channel *Don't Miss This* with Emily Belle Freeman and is the author of many religious books, including *Ites: An Illustrated Guide to the People in the Book of Mormon*; *The Peter Potential*; and *Almighty: How the Most Powerful Being in the Universe Is Also Your Loving Father*. Follow him on Instagram @mrdavebutler.